W9-AAH-258

THE DAY THEY
TOOK THE CHILDREN

THE DAY THEY
TOOK THE CHILDREN

BEN WICKS

Stoddart

HRH PRINCESS ELIZABETH'S ADDRESS TO THE NATION'S CHILDREN

The following broadcast was made by Her Royal Highness Princess Elizabeth, aged fourteen, on BBC Radio's *Children's Hour* on 13 October 1940:

In wishing you all good evening, I know that I am speaking to friends and companions who have shared with my sister and myself many a happy *Children's Hour*. Thousands of you in this country have had to leave your homes and be separated from your fathers and mothers. My sister Margaret Rose and I feel so much for you, as we know from experience what it means to be away from those we love most of all. To you living in new surroundings we send a message of true sympathy, and at the same time we would like to thank the kind people who have welcomed you to their homes in the country.

All of us children who are still at home think continually of our friends and relations who have gone overseas to find a wartime home and a kindly welcome in Canada, Australia, New Zealand, South Africa and the United States of America.

My sister and I feel we know quite a lot about these countries. Our father and mother have so often talked to us of their visits to different parts of the world, so it is not difficult for us to picture the sort of life you are all leading, and to think of all the new sights you must be seeing and the adventures you must be having, but I am sure that you too are often thinking of the old country. I know you won't forget us. It is just that we are not forgetting you, but want on behalf of all the children at home to send you our love and best wishes, to you and your kind hosts as well.

Princess Elizabeth and Princess Margaret at the microphone.

Before I finish, I can truthfully say to you all that we children at home are full of cheerfulness and courage. We are trying to do all we can to help our gallant sailors, soldiers and airmen. And we are trying, too, to bear our own share of the danger and sadness of war. We know, every one of us, that in the end, all will be well, for God will care for us and give us victory and peace. And though peace comes, remember, it will be for us, the children of today, to make the world of tomorrow a better and happier place.

My sister is by my side and we are both going to say good night to you. Come on Margaret. . .

[Margaret:] Good night children.

[Elizabeth:] Good night and good luck to you all.

Copyright © 1989 by Ben Wicks

All rights reserved. No part of this publication may be reproduced or transmitted in any form or by any means, electronic or mechanical, including photocopy, recording, or any information storage and retrieval system, without permission in writing from the publisher.

First published in 1989 by
Stoddart Publishing Co. Limited
34 Lesmill Road
Toronto, Canada
M3B 2T6

Published in the United Kingdom by Bloomsbury Publishing Limited

CANADIAN CATALOGUING IN PUBLICATION DATA

Wicks, Ben
    The day they took the children

ISBN 0-7737-2362-5

1. World War, 1939-45 – Evacuation of civilians – Great Britain
2. World War, 1939-45 – Children – Great Britain
3. World War, 1939-45 – Personal narratives, British
4. Children – Great Britain – History – 20th Century
I. Title

D810.C4W52   1989   940.53′161′0941   C89-094422-9

PICTURE CREDITS

BBC Hulton Picture Library: front cover *inset*, back cover, 3, 16 *bottom*, 24 *bottom left*, 26 *centre*, 48-9, 55 *bottom*, 75 *top*, 99, 145, 147, 156, 157, 161; Canadian Broadcasting Corporation: 154, 155; *Illustrated London News* Picture Library: 5; The Trustees of the Imperial War Museum: front cover *main picture*, 4, 9, 14, 20 *top right*, 23 *bottom right*, 24 *bottom right*, 38, 43, 51, 52, 54 *centre & bottom*, 55 *top*, 57, 60 *top*, 64, 66 *top*, 67, 70, 71, 78 *top*, 80, 81, 85, 89, 95, 110, 113, 120-1, 124, 130-1, 133 *left*, 135, 139, 140 *top*, 149, 160 *top*, 163, 168 *top*, 169; Popperfoto: 10, 12-13, 15, 16 *top left & top right*, 17 *top*, 19, 20 *top left & bottom*, 23 *top left & bottom*, 24 *top*, 26 *top*, 27, 30-1, 33, 34, 37, 40, 44, 46, 46-7, 60 *bottom*, 65, 66 *bottom*, 69, 72, 75 *bottom*, 78 *bottom*, 83, 87, 93 *top*, 108-9, 112, 114, 123, 132, 136, 140 *bottom*, 142-3, 144, 152, 158-9, 165, 167, 168 *centre & bottom*; Popperfoto/Saidman: 63; Sport & General Press Agency: 22, 25; John Topham Picture Library: 17 *bottom*, 26 *bottom*, 28, 54 *top*, 55, 93 *bottom*, 98, 118, 127.
All other pictures kindly lent by the ex-evacuees whose letters appear in this book

Designed by Roy Williams and Laurence Bradbury
Picture research by Jenny de Gex
Typeset by SX Composing Ltd
Printed and bound in the United Kingdom

CONTENTS

FOREWORD

Many of the ex-evacuees were in tears as they stepped on to the platform at Marylebone Station on 1 September 1988. It was almost fifty years since, as children, they had lined up on railway platforms all over the country for quite a different reason. The reunion to launch my book *No Time to Wave Goodbye* had brought 700 men and women together from all parts of Britain to the London railway station to relive the moment on 1 September 1939 when, as German troops crossed the border into Poland, the first of more than three million evacuees, most aged between five and fourteen, began their journey from the bomb-threatened inner cities to the safety of the countryside.

Intended as a pre-emptive move before the enemy started bombing civilian populations, the evacuation had a lifelong effect on those who took part. 'We would never be the same again,' said movie actor Michael Caine, who as an eight-year-old boy had left his home in the East End of London.

Amba and Ann James from Holloway, in London, agreed, recalling the months when they had survived on blackberries and on scraps left over from their foster family's meals. The reunion brought back many memories – some harsh, some joyful – for everyone who attended, and in whose lives evacuation had played such an important part.

Two friends rediscovered each other as they stood in the shadow of an old steam engine that had been brought to the scene by British Rail and now stood silent by the platform. Shirley Shine and Olive Gardner had both been evacuated from the same North London school to Wisbech, in Cambridgeshire. Olive Gardner had stayed only six weeks, however. 'My mother could not stick it,' she said.

Members of the Women's Royal Volunteer Service, dressed in old wartime uniforms, distributed 'iron rations', much the same as had been given out in 1939. On a small stage, a band played melodies from the war, as singer Lee Leslie, dressed in the army uniform of the day, sang the lyrics made famous by Vera Lynn. Soon everyone was joining in the wartime songs.

Kenneth Barber, porter for a London market, stopped singing long enough to remember how he had been taken from his home in the East End of London to a village near Doncaster. 'They just wanted the allowance they were given for keeping me,' he said of his foster parents. 'All the food went to their children. It got so bad that when the mother went out she would measure the loaf of bread with a piece of string.'

For many of the evacuees, that trip to the countryside so long ago

One of Southern Railway's evacuation posters, which in the late summer of 1939 was displayed at stations throughout the south of England. Many of the ex-evacuees at the 1988 reunion at Marylebone had, 49 years earlier, travelled on the very trains that disrupted normal services in September 1939.

EVACUATION

OF

WOMEN AND CHILDREN

FROM LONDON, Etc.

FRIDAY, 1st SEPTEMBER.

Up and Down business trains as usual, with few exceptions.

Main Line and Suburban services will be curtailed while evacuation is in progress during the day.

SATURDAY & SUNDAY,

SEPTEMBER 2nd & 3rd.

The train service will be exactly the same as on Friday.

Remember that there will be very few Down Mid-day business trains on Saturday.

SOUTHERN RAILWAY

Printed in Great Britain by McCorquodale & Co. Ltd., London. 40283.

had been a first. Mary Speaight, who as a young art teacher had taken her class of children to Somerset, recalled, 'Many were so used to chips that it took a long time to persuade them to eat fresh vegetables.'

Several of the ex-evacuees who were at the reunion that day later wrote to say how much they had enjoyed it. For Wendy Gibbs, however, it turned out to be a day of both laughter and sadness:

What can I say about September 1st, 1988? I'm sure it was the best day I've ever had. I met such a lot of lovely people and we all had lots of happy and sad experiences to share. We are keeping in touch and can't wait for September 1st, 1989 for the big one.

But, Ben, sad news for me. My beautiful Auntie Olive, who was my wartime mummy, died at 12.30 p.m. while we were all enjoying ourselves. But do you know, Ben, I said to my two sisters, Auntie Olive is here with us.

I lost a true friend and I will miss her.

Audrey Webb didn't make it to the party, although she had an invitation:

Part of me wanted to and the other part just could not face it alone. Both my sisters, who were part of my story, died of cancer almost a year ago now, just five weeks apart. I had the privilege of being with one during her last two weeks and I know we spoke of your book. On one of her good days I said, 'You and I have a date next year to see the book launched,' and she said, 'That will be lovely.' I knew it would never be and I'm sure she did also. Isn't it amazing how we all kid one another – never the real truth at a time like this. So I'm afraid when the time came I just could not face it alone, too many memories.

I wish Audrey had come to the evacuee reunion. She would have seen that she was not alone. She was one of a whole army of men and women, some of whom now appeared, as if from out of the past, to remind us of an event that had been buried for almost fifty years. Their experiences often overshadowed by the more glamorous events of the war, these were the forgotten many – the evacuees.

To the hundreds of thousands of Audreys and Harrys and Olives and Alberts, this book is dedicated with love.

Audrey Nolder (now Webb) with her foster parents, Emily and Martin Field, and her eldest sister, Patricia (standing, centre), 1940.

Opposite: The first school to get evacuation under way 1 September 1939 was Myrdle School in London's East End, where children began assembling at 5.30 a.m.

!
SAYING
GOODBYE

It had been a wonderful summer. One of the best in years. The last thing on the minds of many living in Britain in 1939 was war. Yet as the summer began to to fade, events were taking place in Europe that were to change the lives of most of those who called Britain their home.

On the morning of Friday 1 September 1939, hundreds of thousands of children left their homes for school, only to find themselves being told to return home, pack a bag and return to school ready for evacuation to the countryside.

Jo Eckersley (née Burke), who was living in Salford, Manchester, recalls:

My brother Peter was four years older than I, and I was approximately ten years old when I was evacuated to Blackpool. I can still bring to mind the vision of my mother running after me as I marched with the rest of my school to the railway station – to give me some handkerchiefs which she said I didn't have (I had at least twenty packed in my pillow case). She was crying, and of course that was just an excuse to see me again.

Some children, such as Pamela Picknell (now Greenough), had been prepared for evacuation for some time before the actual outbreak of war:

I was eight years old when war broke out and was attending Holy Trinity School in Sloane Square, London. For a week or two before war was declared we had had packed suitcases and haversacks stored at school.

Left: *Waiting to be evacuated.*
Opposite: *Blackboard instructions at Southwark Central School, London.*

Clothing required.

1. Overcoat or mackintosh

2. In Haversack: One vest
   Also, Night attire.   · shirt with collar
                             · pair of pants
     Coat.   · pullover or
     Plimsolls.   jersey
     Towel.   · pair of knickers
     Soap.   Handkerchief
     Face-cloth.   Two pairs of socks a
     Tooth brush & if   stockings
   poss: boots or shoes.

   ――――――――――――――――――――――

   Gas Mask to be carried.

All boys should bring
enough food for the day

Suggestions
   Sandwiches (egg or ch...
   Packets of nuts or seedles
                      rais...
   Dry biscuits with cheese
   Barley sugar (is better tha
                   chocolate)
   Apple, orange.

Checking luggage labels . . .

. . . awaiting instructions . . .

. . . endlessly queuing . . .

. . . still waiting . . .

. . and off to the station at last!

On the Monday after war was declared we met at the school and were marched off to Victoria Station and taken to Egham, where the billeting officer took us around and settled us with various families.

I was at first with a fairly elderly couple, who were kind to me, but because the husband didn't like fidgety children, I ate alone in the kitchen. This was an advantage to me, as it enabled me to read at the table, something I had not been allowed to do at home and which I really enjoyed.

When Rosemary Richman (now Johnson) was evacuated, it was her mother she was going to miss most of all:

My mother had practically brought us up, as my dad gambled most of his wages (he was a bus driver) and philandered with women; he was also an ex-soldier and in the reserves, so he was called up straight away. My mother always worked to keep us – three of us, my brother John, aged eleven, me in the middle, Rosemary, aged nine, and my little sister, Sylvie, aged five. As I say, my mother had mostly been charring, and when war broke out she was working in a nursing home, but soon afer Christmas 1939 she was in a munitions factory called Reid and Sigrist at Shannon Corner, which was about five miles from where we lived in Wimbledon.

Because of my dad, we were always moving, and twice in my childhood I can remember the bailiffs coming and taking all the furniture away, so off we'd go again to another rented room.

In early 1939 my maternal grandad died and left my mother £300, which she put down on a little terraced house, 24 William Road, Wimbledon, and what's more incredible (for those days, anyway) is that the Halifax Building Society actually gave her the mortgage!

The coming of the war was really the making of my mum. She had a permanent roof over her head, and with my dad being back in the Army, she had a regular allowance – and a well-paid job making gyros for aircraft, or in some cases, she said, parts were sent back from crashed planes that sometimes had the blood still splattered from dead pilots, to be repaired.

My mother (who is still alive and living up here in Sheffield where my husband and I finally settled) says that it was on the 4th September that we were evacuated.

My brother, sister and I assembled at Dundonald Road School, which we were attending at the time, and marched to the station; I don't think we had much idea of what was going on, but I do remember that we were very excited. There were hundreds of us and a lot of mothers crying.

Left: *An ARP notice showing the way to the local gas-mask fitting centre.*
Below: *Gas-mask drill for under-fives at a London County Council residential school near Windsor.*

Our names were pinned to our coats, and we all had a carrier bag with various items which we were dying to delve into the moment we were away from authority – but to our disgust we found they were all tins!

As an eight-year-old, Valerie Gibbs (the late Valerie Benest) was among the children who assembled in the hall of St George's School in London on the day before war was declared:

Both my parents were at home in Linden Gardens, W2; my dad, being an older age group, was not called up for service until 1941. I was their only surviving child; two brothers had died previously.

I remember that my mother had marked all my clothes by sewing tapes with my name in India ink. She had spent hours sewing a tape to every article of clothing.

At the assembly we were given tags to wear, and also had our gas-masks over our shoulders. We didn't know where we were going. Being very shy, I didn't ask any questions, and went along with the crowd of jostling kids, some crying, some fooling around, some quiet and some putting on a brave front.

We were then marched down to Notting Hill Gate tube station, and eventually boarded a special train which took us to Ealing station, where we boarded a Great Western train which arrived at Chippenham, Wiltshire. After a short bus trip we were dropped off at Lacock, a small village about thirteen miles from Bath, in Somerset.

Reginald Slee was twelve, and lived with his mother, father, brother and two younger sisters close to the Arsenal football ground in North London. Soon after the declaration of war, his parents were notified that the school he was attending, Blackstock Road School in Finsbury Park, was to be evacuated:

We were told to muster at Montem Street School, which is off Tollington Park in North London, which was more central for all the schools in the surrounding area I suppose. I arrived at this school with my mother, who was seeing us off, and my two sisters, who were going on the evacuation scheme with me. My elder sister was ten years old and my younger sister was six years old. My brother did not go, because he was nearly fourteen years of age. That was the age for starting work at that time.

When we arrived at the school there were about three or four hundred other children from other schools there. We were taken into classrooms and given name-tags which we had to put around our necks, tied with string. They told us we were going to be evacuated out of London for fear

rriving at school,
with bags and tags.
Opposite are the four
Brown children from
Clerkenwell Green,
London: William (9),
Margaret (4), John
(1) and Eileen (10).
Their knapsacks were
made by their father.

*King's Cross Station,
October 1939.*

of the bombing, but they did not tell us where we were going. We were
taken by coach to Paddington Station.

It was pandemonium at the station. You could not move for people
and children, like coming out of a football match. Anyhow, we were put
on a train with our luggage, which consisted of a small suitcase. The train
was packed with children leaning out of the windows waving to their
parents goodbye. Some were crying, as they did not want to leave them;
it was a sad sight. I cannot remember if I shed a few tears or not. We did
not know if and when we would see our parents again.

The train pulled out of the station and we were on our way to a destination unknown to us at the time. We were travelling on the train for about
eight or nine hours, in which time we were supplied with sandwiches and
tea to eat and drink. It was, or seemed, a slow train, run by coal and water
– a steam train. It had to stop two or three times to fill up with water
before it arrived at our destination.

...ove: Notices at ...aring Cross Station ...nouncing changes ... railway services ...ring the weekend of ... great evacuation. ...ght: Children being ...acuated from ...istol. ...low: Mothers and ...ir babies waiting to ...ard trains at ...ctoria Station.

Left: *A mother's and daughter's parting hug before the train pulls out of the station.*
Far left: *A boy and a girl kiss their baby brother goodbye before leaving London.*
Opposite: *A boy from Park Walk School, Chelsea gets a farewell kiss from his dad.*
Below: *Infant evacuees with their village foster mothers.*

Left: *Mothers have a last word with their children before the train leaves Euston.*
Below: *A final wave as the evacuees set off for an 'unknown destination'.*

Left: *A welcome break in the journey for much-needed refreshments.*
Opposite: *A novel way to travel. Preparing for evacuation from Gravesend, Kent.*

Not everyone went by road or rail. Anxious to evacuate as many as possible in the short time they judged was available, the Government pressed all means of transportation into service. Joan Butler (now Foster), who was almost twelve when war was declared, was living near Gravesend, Kent, and was evacuated by boat:

On that same day I think it was, my mother and two older sisters (who had jobs) escorted me about 5 a.m. (my father was too upset to come to see me off), complete with gas-mask, suitcase and small knapsack containing rations for two days (corned beef, Ryvita, chocolate I remember). And a label on my coat.

We walked the almost empty streets about three miles to West Street Pier, Gravesend. That was a deep-water long pier where pleasure

Above: *Lining up for evacuation by boat from Gravesend, Kent.*
Right: *Laden with its cargo of mothers and children, the boat sails from Gravesend on its way down the Thames estuary and up the coast.*

steamers called to and from London on day trips to Margate, Ramsgate etc. I believe our boat was the *Royal Daffodil*.

In our group of schools were the two grammar schools, a boys' Roman Catholic school and some other schools. We all waved madly to our families on shore, though they were too small to identify. For myself, I thoroughly enjoyed the voyage round the coast up to Lowestoft [in Suffolk]. Many pupils and some mistresses were seasick, but I loved the trip.

Although more than 1.3 million children were evacuated in the first week of the war, many parents decided – often at the last minute – to keep their children at home. Eight-year-old Ivy Dunwoodie (now Parker) and her six-year-old brother 'were nearly evacuees from Liverpool':

Our bags were packed and we were going to Wales, which was a foreign country to us. I remember going around all our aunties and our nanny (grandmother) and the neighbours, collecting huge kisses, money and sweets.

We were to leave on a bus from Upper Park Street School on Monday morning. Imagine the shock, coming downstairs Sunday morning to hear my mum crying, 'They're not going. No one's murdering my children.' She and Dad, who was home on leave, were reading the *News of the World* about the murdered bodies of these little brothers who had been taken in by a shepherd and his wife. They were found on the moors.

It was the saddest day of my life, going with Mum to Upper Park Street School on the Monday to say we weren't going, and waving goodbye and shouting, 'Ta ra!' to the busload of siren-suited kids with their gas-masks, all waving excitedly to their weeping families.

My nanny gave us a hug and a kiss and said, 'Thank God, he's answered my prayers. I didn't want you to go anyway.'

Eileen Challis (née Williamson), whose father had died just a few months before the outbreak of war, remembers that her mother was not anxious for the family to be split:

I was only six years old when all the children were being evacuated. My father had died in March 1939. So there was my mother, me and my three elder brothers. Two of my brothers joined up, one in the Army, one in the Royal Air Force. My eldest brother was mentally retarded, so was at home with Mother and myself. Well, a letter came for us to be evacuated. My mother said, 'We stay at home together, in case the boys come home and don't know where we are.'

2 'IT WAS LIKE A CATTLE MARKET'

Most of the children boarded trains that rattled their way to a mysterious land that few of them had ever seen. As the trains squealed into the country stations, thousands of tiny faces pressed their noses against the carriage windows, anxious to catch a glimpse of their new home.

The locals, many of whom had waited hours for the children to arrive, followed the billeting officers to schools and church halls for their first meeting with the children. It was a time that would be stamped on the minds of evacuees for ever. Many of them stood and waited to be picked out, hoping that their 'borrowed' parents would show them love and kindness. Others, like Pat Malone (now Reesor), were walked from door to door in the search for someone willing to take them in:

September 1st, 1939 changed my whole life. I will never forget the evacuation.

I can remember that for the week of August 28th, 1939, every day we all went to school with our name-tags on, carrying our suitcases. My mother would say every day, 'Goodbye girl,' and cry, thinking that I would not be coming home that night. On the Friday morning she said, 'Goodbye girl, see you tonight . . .'

That Friday is etched in my memory. I remember the whole school walking along East Ham High Street with our placard saying 'Altmore Ave Public School', carrying all our worldly possessions (or so it seemed). All the mothers and fathers standing at the side of the road, crying and waving. Getting to East Ham station and being loaded in trains in packs. Arriving at Marlow on Thames (which really isn't very far by today's standards), going to the reception centre, then being walked in a 'crocodile line' along streets in this beautiful little town, with the person in charge knocking on doors and saying something like, 'Mrs Brown, how many did you want?' and some of the local children saying to their parents, 'Mum, have that one.'

I can remember the Sunday morning, September 3rd, 1939, when war was declared, and how we all cried.

The sad thing was that my mother died in February 1940, leaving me an orphan (my father having died just before the war). I never had a home in London after that.

June Robinson (now Swindle) was evacuated with her younger sister:

I clearly remember being hugged and kissed goodbye, half a crown being pressed into my hand (which was a fortune compared to my usual

*Above: A group of forlorn-looking little evacuees waiting to be collected – and obviously feeling a long way from home.
Right: Another busload of youngsters arrives in the countryside – to the apparent fascination of the local residents.*

threepenny-bit spending money), and my mother's last words were, 'Look after your little sister and remember, you've *got* to stay together!'

Then off we went, a busload of screaming, yelling, waving – and some of the very young ones crying – evacuees, off on a great adventure. The bus stopped at a little church and we could see a small crowd of people, mostly women. Some of the children were told to get off the bus. I was

*In Beaconsfield,
Buckinghamshire,
evacuees from London
wait for the bus that
will take them to their
billets.*

sitting at the back with my six-year-old sister beside me hanging on for dear life.

I heard a young woman in the crowd say to someone in charge that she wanted a little girl about five or six. Immediately I pushed my sister under the seat, but of course they had a list of names and ages, and they soon came looking for her. However, remembering my mother's words, I said, 'She can't go without me.' That didn't go over too well, I can tell you, as this young woman, who loved on sight my pretty red-headed, brown-eyed, dimpled, sweet little sister, wanted no part of her gangly, freckle-faced premenstrual twelve-year-old sister.

However, a compromise was reached when the young woman's 60-year-old mother said she would take me, and as she lived very near her daughter, it worked out very well. I stayed with her and her husband – who worked in a local mine – for a few months, and I was very happy there. They had raised five daughters of their own, and I learnt a lot from them. To this day I can close my eyes and see and almost smell the fresh bread and brown cakes she used to bake every week.

Eileen Stevens (now Watkins) was ten years old when war broke out, and living in Shoeburyness, in Essex. Nine months later she found herself nearly two hundred miles away from home:

My father had died in January 1939, my brother was in the regular Army and my sister was enlisted in the ATS. This left my widowed mother to decide what was best for the 'baby' of the family. She grudgingly came to the conclusion that evacuation was for me!

About 160 of us kids were taken or dragged to the school assembly hall, suitcases in hand, name-tags pinned to our clothing and a small brown cardboard box containing a gas-mask slung over our shoulders. Fortunately it was to remain in that box for the duration of the war.

Sad farewells over, we were bundled into the waiting buses to be taken we knew not where! I remember little of that journey as I, like many others, was too busy crying. One thing that does stick in my mind is the dedicated teachers trying to cheer us up and organizing a sing-along. Whenever I hear children singing 'Ten Green Bottles' or 'One Man Went to Mow' I remember that day!

After several comfort stops and head-counting, we finally arrived at our destination – Buxton, Derbyshire. Tired, miserable and very hungry, we alighted from the buses and were taken into a large hall where we were given a meal. Later we were told that all foster billets had been filled by children from Manchester so we had to spend that first night on the hall floor. Next morning we were taken to the village of Castleton, which nestles at the foot of the Pennines. Here we were ushered into a hall and lined up to be 'chosen'. What a terrible ordeal that was. I liken it to Hansel and Gretel: I thought we were to be prodded to see if we were meaty enough to be put in the pot! How wrong I was.

My schoolfriend Jean and I were standing side by side feeling very bedraggled and sorry for ourselves when a tall, slim, elderly lady stopped in front of us. She said, 'Eee, tha looks sad and lonely lasses. Would you like to come and live with us?' We said, 'Yes please,' wondering why she talked funny! After the formalities we became the foster children of Mr and Mrs Hare of Market Place, Castleton.

We walked the short distance from the hall to their quaint home. We were greeted by the excited barking of two Pomeranian dogs and the aroma of freshly baked bread. Before we were allowed to taste the bread we had to have a bath in a huge zinc tub in front of the fire. There was always a fire, as this was used for cooking and baking. After our bath, we were shown our bedroom, in which was a huge double bed, so high that we had to stand on a box to get into it, with a feather mattress and eiderdown. (These proved to be invaluable during the cold, snowy winter.) We were then given huge chunks of the fresh bread and cheese. Maybe they were trying to fatten us up!

Mr and Mrs Hare were retired publicans with no children of their own. Mrs Hare was very fond of children, and being a foster mother brought out the best in her. She would take us for walks at weekends to explore the beautiful countryside and the numerous caverns and caves in the district. Mr Hare was very kind, but more interested in his dogs and dog shows. I did not realize until many years later that Mrs Hare was seventy years old when she took us under her wing. She could walk and climb those hills as well as we could.

I spent a happy nine months in Castleton. In March 1941 Jean and I were told that we had passed our Scholarship Exam and would be going to high school. We were both loath to leave this place and these kindly folk, but our mothers thought it best that we take advantage of the scholarship and further our education.

Knowing that some of the children had been ill-treated, I found the prospect of a new billet rather disturbing – but I needn't have worried. In June 1941 I was escorted by a teacher to New Mills, near Stockport, to start at my new school. Once again it was into a church hall to be chosen, and once again I was one of the lucky ones.

Edward and Ellen Winterbottom, a young couple with a three-year-old daughter, Irene, took me into their home and hearts. Uncle and Auntie, as I called them from that day on, had a delightful home at the top of a very steep hill looking down on to the town and valley. I hated that hill in winter, and it was the only way to school! Auntie was an excellent cook and needlewoman, and I have her to thank for teaching me to sew and cook. When Auntie was pregnant with her second child she was very sick, and my mother offered to come and help out. To my delight, she stayed for ten months and was godmother to the new baby, Gordon. Uncle was a jolly man, placid and with a great love for children. He was a truck-driver and worked long hours. His hobby was breeding budgies.

Six months before the war ended, the board of governors of the convent said it was safe for me to return home. Sadly, I said my farewells to Auntie, Uncle and the children, promising to keep in contact. It was wonderful to be back home with my family. (The board of governors was proved wrong. Two weeks after I started school, it was hit by a bomb in a night raid. The school was badly damaged, and five ATS women staying in a house nearby were killed.)

Elizabeth Byron (now Russ) soon discovered that she was far from welcome in her new home:

I was twelve and my brother ten when we were evacuated from Herne Hill, London, out to Buckley Wharf [near Chester]. We arrived at the place after what seemed a very long trip. We were brought into the town centre sometime in the late afternoon. Quite a few of the kids were taken almost right away by various couples. When they had left with their foster parents there was a small group of us left. The remaining people seemed to have to make a choice of children they wanted to take. My brother was taken by a couple of elderly ladies; they didn't want the responsibility of myself, as girls of that age in those years were considered hard to handle.

Gradually children were picked out, and myself and a couple of other girls the same age were left waiting. Some sort of fight between a lady and

a councillor went on while we waited, and I remember hearing the lady saying she didn't really want to take anyone, especially a girl. It was somehow sorted out after a little while; the other girls went off and I was told to go with the lady.

I don't remember her name, but I do remember she asked my name and told me to follow her. Carrying my little suitcases, I tried to walk with her, and out of nervousness walked chattering about everything and anything. She never spoke to me, apart from asking my name in those first few minutes. We finally arrived at her home. She showed me to a small room and told me to wash and get down to supper or tea-time as soon as I could. It was the start of a very bad experience that for a long time I never let on about.

She constantly told me girls weren't to be trusted, so I was never allowed out after school hours. When my parents visited she couldn't have been nicer, always praising me for being a well-behaved child, never any trouble. My parents brought me small presents; when they left,

Children from London's East End, on their way to Kings Langley, Hertfordshire by bus, stop in Watford to eat their sandwiches.

Left: *A nurse
examines children's
health cards on the
train as they travel
from Bristol to
Kingsbridge, Devon.*
Right: *At Kingsbridge
station, education and
billeting officers check
lists of schools and
billets.*

things were taken away from me, not to be seen again. When my parents weren't around, she let me know in no uncertain way that just because she had been made to take a child in, it didn't mean she had to be nice to me. She made me feel really miserable.

Things went on, but then with one incident it finished. My schoolwork had begun to go down, and teachers had noticed I went very quiet whereas I had been a bit of a chatterbox. The incident that brought things into the open happened when all of a sudden I started menstruating. I had been told by my mother what to expect and what to do if my periods came on, but like girls all over I felt a little scared.

I got out of bed one morning to find blood on the sheets, and I went running to tell the lady and to ask for a pad or cloth. All I got was screamed at, called a dirty pig, put into the bedroom, given a cloth, pins and a piece of elastic and told to see to myself. She seemed disgusted with me.

The carrying on really got me upset and it took me a while to see to myself, with a lot of crying in between. I finally managed to get things in order, and went to breakfast after washing and dressing.

The lady berated me all through breakfast, also letting me know she hadn't wanted a girl anyway. Too much trouble. After the crying she told me to get off to school. Well, as you can imagine, by the time I got to school, my face and eyes were badly swollen and I was still crying, I couldn't stop. I was sent to the headmaster's room and then they brought the school nurse in. She and the headmaster asked what was wrong and everything came out. It was looked into, and evidently with questions she gradually admitted to her attitude.

She had been reluctant to take any of those kids from London, and when told she had to, determined she didn't have to like the idea or the child she took in. I've never forgotten her, even though I don't remember her name.

After a couple of days, still with the lady, my parents were brought

down to speak to the school. They were asked if they wanted me to stay in Buckley Wharf. They decided that seeing raids were still going on in London it might be better to see if relatives in Chester would take my mother, brother and myself in. This is what we did till the end of the war – lived in Chester.

Terry Law moved a number of times from one billet to another:

I was five years old when the war started and was evacuated with Lavender Hill School, Battersea, down to Liss, in Hampshire. I went with my auntie, who was only eight years older than I was. I can remember the label in the lapel, and pulling out of Clapham Junction with all the other kids.

I can recollect being sorted out in the playground of the little school in Liss (still there, of course) and being picked out by 'posh' people and feeling like a sheep on market day. For the period I was there we had several billets, all of which, like the school, are still there. I still drive past those places for another look after all these years.

For Sidney Chapman, 'evacuation proved to be a very positive experience':

In 1939 I was a 17-year-old sixth-former at the Plaistow Secondary School in East London, not far from the dock area. In the expectation that this area would be a prime target for German air raids, plans were made for the evacuation of our school when the outbreak of war seemed imminent. All children whose parents had given permission for them to be evacuated were notified to report to school on August 31st, 1939, to get instructions with regard to the evacuation procedures and to go through the evacuation drill.

Next day the real thing took place. About 300 children, gas-masks slung over their shoulders, and carrying a bare minimum of baggage, wound their way a couple of miles to Plaistow station and boarded a train for 'destination unknown'.

After a number of hours heading west from London, we discovered we had arrived in Weymouth, Dorset. Local volunteers were at a reception centre doing their best to arrange billeting for these homeless kids. It wasn't long before a number of us were hustled into a lorry and one or two or three at a time were dropped off at the homes of people who had expressed a willingness to help.

Perhaps we were more fortunate than many others, because my younger brother (aged nine) and I were placed in a home where we were immediately accepted as part of the family.

On Sunday September 3rd we all listened to Neville Chamberlain report on the radio that war had been declared. And so started a most memorable and eventful year as evacuees.

Word somehow was sent around to all the billets that we should report for school next morning in the buildings associated with a church in Weymouth. It was only then that it was learned that half of the schoolchildren had been loaded on a different train and had landed up in Wellington, Somerset.

Arrangements were quickly made for the 'other half' to be transferred to Weymouth so that the school could function as a unit. Only many years later did we appreciate the difficulties faced by the school's teachers in trying to re-establish a school in very difficult circumstances. The co-operation shown by the local people was really tremendous. The local grammar school agreed that it would go on a shift system and allow us to use their school in the afternoons. In the mornings our classes were held in all sorts of odd places.

In addition to the normal school curriculum, through the fine efforts of the staff we were able to pursue many of the usual extracurricular activities such as sports, choirs, orchestra and field trips. Over and above these we also had a scout troop, numerous school outings to local places of interest, plus the anything-but-normal involvement in digging air-raid trenches on the school playing field.

A group of schoolboys is ushered into a distribution centre.

Margaret Trayling (née Crawford) has written a poem about her life as an evacuee:

We went to school one summer's day
With cases and our bags
They said, 'You're going on a trip
Without your mums and dads.'

We stood there all together
With labels on our coats
And off we walked to the station
Like a herd of innocent goats.

We said goodbye to our parents
Wondering why they cried
Not to know, when we came back
A few of them had died.

We loved the great big steam train
And laughed excitedly
I wondered where we were going
They did say by the sea.

We got out at the end of the line
Now this – this wasn't the same
The platform was full of strangers
It wasn't a funny game.

We marched off in one big line
To the local school they took
And there we sat and waited
While people came to look.

They picked us out, as if cattle
'I'll have that one, no that one there,'
This went on for hours long
Our feelings they did not care.

If you had angelic looks
Then you got picked quite quick
They took one look at me and thought,
'That one looks oh so sick.'

I was fearful and very frightened
Well I wasn't very old
And it had been such a long day
Lonely, and getting cold.

The day went on, the children went
They went in twos and threes
I was getting nervous now
And trembling at my knees.

We were the very last there
All the children gone
This lady came and looked at us
I needed to belong.

The lady must have looked and seen
The sadness in my eyes
She said, 'All right, I'll take them –
But I did want two same size.'

And so this lady took us home
Gave us cake and teas
To a house full of strangers
And these we had to please.

We had to live with this family
But oh, we picked up fleas
Most of the children got them
We were the evacuees.

Frances L. Rubens (née Goodman) also looks back through verse:

At aged 7 one is full of joy
Whether you are girl or boy,
As children, learning words can be fun
Even the word WAR can seem to be one,
Air raid, bombs and shelter too
For a 7-year-old these don't conjure up
'Things' to do.
Evacuee is a word I heard many times in '39
And to this day, brings memories
Which are not so fine.
A long train ride full of tears,
Labels on coats, gas-mask around the neck
Added to the fears
Arrival at a strange place, with fate unknown
Made this 7-year-old feel very much alone.
Grown-ups checked us out, with much
'Looking down the nose',
Perhaps they thought evacuees had horns
. . . do you suppose?
Everyone had been 'chosen' 'cept my sister and me,
'Good, they'll let me go home now,' I thought with glee
But that was not to be
A lady stepped out of the gloom to claim,
'I will give these children a room.'
Time passed, the life of an evacuee remained the same,
Many new places and people were seen,
But this little girl dreamed not of sugar-plum fairies
In her dream
But of a place where love abounds
That one special place she called
HOME

Joan Giles was twelve when she was evacuated from her Manchester home on 1 September 1939. She and her schoolmates left school in a procession, straggling along the streets with their duffel bags and gas-masks, and were put on a train bound for a small village called Marple, in Cheshire:

It was only ten miles away from Manchester, but to us it was the country and a big adventure.

Evacuees in Dartington, Devon, on their way to school.

Buses took us to a church hall, where we were given a snack, then had to wait on the church steps while we were looked over by the village people waiting to pick us out.

Along with another girl (about ten years old) I was chosen by an older couple, who then took us in their car to their home. A car was something only 'well-off' people had, so it was very exciting.

They lived in a lovely large home not too far from the railway station, with a beautiful garden, both front and back. Also in the family was a son – he must have been in his twenties – who worked at the same bank in Manchester that his father did. To round out the occupants of the house were a maid-cook and a chauffeur-gardener (the latter did not live in).

The maid looked after us and we spent the time in the large kitchen at the back of the house, but we had a large front bedroom, looking over a park, and our own wash-basin. I only remember once eating in the dining room with the family, and I was never invited to the lounge.

We had to be in early and used to look out of our bedroom window at our friends, still having fun on the swings, and feel very envious. Mr Taylor used to bring us colouring books and crayons, but at 13 (almost) I wasn't too interested in them. They must have been very good people to take us, but really didn't know what to do with us and it was mainly the maid who looked after us.

My mother used to come on the weekends and we would go into the village to the church hall where we could get something to eat or drink. Parents just came up for the day.

I didn't care for Mrs Taylor very much, and when she criticized my mother for not making me wear long black wool stockings (I didn't want them) and a couple more things I cannot remember, it didn't make my feelings change for her for the better, so I asked to be moved.

Four children are delivered to their billet.

With her brother John, aged eleven, and sister Sylvie, aged five, Rose-mary Richman (now Johnson) was evacuated by train from Wimble-don in South London, to Chichester, in Sussex:

As we were three poor kids, who had previously only been on a day trip to Southend on the annual Sunday School outing, it was all a big adven-ture! After what seemed like ages at the distribution centre in

Chichester, the three of us were taken to a big posh house, just outside Chichester, in a village called Fishbourne, where an old man lived. (I think he was oriental, or possibly Indian.) He was obviously well off and was obliged to take in evacuees, but I don't think he bargained for the likes of us! Somehow we must have heard someone say that he had pots of gold, because we tore around this big house delving into all the vases and receptacles – to the amazement and horror of the old man's housekeeper. Well, the next day we were taken away and deemed not suitable for such an esteemed billet.

I think the idea had been to keep us three together, but after that we had to split up. I was taken to a Mr and Mrs Hanmore, who had a two-year-old daughter. I was not happy there, as Mr Hanmore was very strict and it was obvious he didn't really want an evacuee. Mrs Hanmore was a very timid woman and I think she was frightened of her humourless husband.

He also couldn't stand boys. As my brother, who was boisterous and a 'show off', was billeted just up the road from me – with a lovely family, a Mrs Geach with lots of children of her own – he used to come and see me, and he was was only allowed in the garden. He'd come and play rough-and-tumble with me and the little girl and cause an awful lot of bother.

Now, I don't know why exactly, because I think I was quite an easy child to bring up – my mother says that I had a happy nature, but on the shy side (I've made up for it since, mind!) – but anyway, I seemed to have quite a few different billets.

I can't remember how long I stayed with the Hanmores or why I left there, but at one time I was billeted in what I regarded as a lovely place, with a lady whose name escapes me, but she had three or four children of her own, one of whom was a girl a little older than me, who got most of our meals, and she would take me into her mum's bedroom where we messed about with make-up, clothes, etc. Her mum would be out every night with various 'uncles' and wear curlers all day, but a very sweet-tempered woman. I never did work out why I had to move on from there!

My mother would come down to see us once a month, and in the summer she would bring a picnic, but this never did seem to go down well with our surrogate families, who always wanted her to stay in their houses instead. This could be very time-consuming as we were split into three billets, and also my mum was a bit unusual and did not like other kids' mums: when confronted with complaints she just retaliated with complete silence, and as we had to go on living there after she had gone back to London it became very fraught at times.

But one lovely summer's day we met her at the station, and the four of us all went on a picnic across some fields where we took off our shoes and

London mothers enjoying the beach on a visit to their evacuated children in Brighton.

socks, and mum took off her stockings and set out our food and we soon got tucked in. I remember to this day, lovely home-made meat pies in little white pots. What we didn't notice until too late was a herd of bullocks slowly coming our way – well, we vaguely saw them on the other side of the stream, but it didn't enter our heads that they would cross. So there we sat eating our food when to our horror we saw the beasts nearly on top of us. Well, we all ran like mad to the perimeter and climbed over the fence, and they devoured everything! And I do mean everything, as when they finally receded back across the stream and we inspected the damage, we found not a trace of our socks or my mum's stockings.

As for schooling, I do know that the three of us must have gone to different ones. I can remember going to the Bishop's palace for some subjects, one being literature; I can recall *A Midsummer Night's Dream* in the grounds of the cathedral; and although I cannot remember it, I must have passed what amounted to the 11-plus, as in 1944 I came back to London and went to the Pelham Road Grammar School.

But the billet I can remember the best was being near the cathedral with a widow and her son and her sister. I wish I could think of their name, but I can't, except the son's name was Arthur and he was a hunch-backed little chap, I should think about forty years of age, who gave piano lessons for a living. This poor little trio lived in a wee terraced house and, when I look back, existed on a pittance. I should have thought that the only reason that they applied for an evacuee was for the ten bob as week!

I look back with so much affection on these three, two elderly women and Arthur. The house was always cold, and poor Arthur, who had his piano in the front parlour (which the front door opened into), always seemed to have a 'dew-drop' on his nose. We had candles to take to bed up the stairs; the access was through a sort of cupboard door leading from the parlour.

Poor Arthur's mother just had a widow's pension, so she and her sister Amy took in washing for a living. Arthur's mother washed for a solicitor, so the copper was lit in the scullery on Monday morning, and starch made, and in would go the solicitor's smalls etc., then second would go in (the same water) Amy's clients', and third would be ours.

When I think of those two poor hardworking souls, it seems their lives were all misery; they always seemed to have their sleeves rolled up and water running down their arms, and red noses. They lived so frugally; the little joint of meat would have to make do for days, and when I look back, I always seem to have been hungry. I was very fond of them, but I never knew what happened to them or kept in touch. Some years ago now (20 or more) I went back to Chichester with my husband, but I could not seem to find this road of terraced houses near the cathedral.

During my stay in Chichester, I don't know how, but I used to go to the house of an old lady, who I think was an authoress. Her name, I re-member quite clearly, was Miss Lefèvre, and I think she spent most of her life in India and had written books about it. She had a housekeeper/companion called Nellie Payne. They befriended me and I loved them both, especially Nellie. They lived in what I think was called a 'triangle' – they have these mostly in cathedral districts, don't they? Or was it a 'qua-drangle'? It could have been.

Well, every Saturday morning I would go down into the cellar of this big old house and pile up all the logs which had just been emptied in, and put them into nice tidy order, for which I was paid threepence (old pence, of course). I remember buying one ounce of wool with this three-pence, bright red. I think it took six ounces to make my first knitted article; it was a cross-over short-sleeved cardigan with a cable up the front!

Gas-masks always at the ready – day and night.

3
LIFE
IN
THE
COUNTRY

Away from the dirt and soot of the cities, the children found a new world to explore.

Sylvia Dilke (now Williams) was five when she left Birmingham to go to Earl Shilton, in Leicestershire, where she stayed for three years:

To go from a town to a countryside where there were cows, sheep and horses, which I never knew about, was a lovely feeling. I think I was too young to appreciate that I was leaving my mother and father and baby sister.

We were all (evacuees) taken to a hostel where we were sorted into age groups. I know I cried brokenhearted when they took my sister to another room.

One thing has stuck in my mind over the years. My dear mother had pinned a ten-shilling note to my vest. It was for pocket money. When I woke up in that strange bedroom the next morning it had gone. I never found out what happened to it.

Anyway, the next morning we were all made to stand to attention in a big hall, and this big woman and a little man picked my sister and me out and we went to live with them. We were with them for about six months, but I don't think the woman had ever been a mother, because she was cruel to my sister and me. We were forever crying, and one day the woman's sister came to see us and asked my sister and me if we would like to go and live with her and her brother. We both said yes, and from then on till the end of the war, I can honestly say, they were the happiest times of my life.

One day when we went to school – it was a lovely little school out in the country, and just off the playground was a farm and there was a big hay-stack – myself and my friends had found an old flagon of ginger beer. During playtime we climbed to the top of the haystack and drank the ginger beer, and we were all drunk. We found out afterwards that the teachers, police, everybody was looking for us. No one thought of looking on top of the haystack. Our teacher, Miss Massey, told us afterwards that about 6 p.m. she heard groans and found us up there. Mind you, we all had a good hiding for it.

Where we lived was a lovely little house in the high street. Outside the back was a lovely garden and an orchard, chickens and an old well that my foster aunt took the water from for everything. Many happy hours my sister and I spent in that garden.

There are numerous tales I could tell. The house where we lived, the front was a cobbler's shop, and whenever I smell leather it takes me back in time. I know my sister and I always had good shoes. My foster uncle always used to talk to us with a mouth full of tacks. I asked him once,

Left: *At their new home on a farm in Dartington, Devon, evacuees take a peek at the pigs.*
Below: *Learning a bit of horse sense in the farmyard.*

Above: *Young Freddie King from Fulham, London finds out where eggs come from!*

'Don't you ever swallow any?' He said, 'No.' It still amazes me how he did it.

We used to skate on the village pond in the depth of winter in our wellies. It wasn't very deep. It was great fun.

Just opposite our house was a lovely little lane, and at the end of it was a baker's shop. My auntie used to tell me after school to go for a loaf and she used to give me two old pennies for going.

I loved reading. My favourite was *Sunny Stories*, and I remember when they were on strike, I pestered that poor lady in the shop for about three weeks. She told me later how relieved she was when the *Sunny Stories* came back in.

One day my sister and I and a few of our friends were walking down a country lane. It was a lovely summer's day. Suddenly my sister shouted, 'There's a German stuck in that tree.' We were all scared and ran to fetch the village policeman. When he came he went up to the tree, and he found it was an old potato bag stuck in the branches. We'd really thought it was a German parachutist. Anyway, the policeman thanked us and said we were good children for reporting the incident.

I am 53 years old now. My foster aunt and uncle died in 1948 and I ·have never been back to Earl Shilton. I wish to keep my happy memories inside me and not spoil them by finding out where we lived has been spoiled beyond all recognition.

Eleanor Merrilees (now Johnstone) grew very fond of the place where she was billeted:

I was evacuated from Felling on Tyne a few months after the war started – I believe it was early summer, 1940 – to a small village in the county of Durham, called Stanhope (pronounced Stanup). I was eight years old at the time.

I remember waiting on the railway platform with many other children and some teachers as chaperones, each with our little gas-mask and suitcases containing the requisite amount of clothing which had to be provided by our families. I don't remember the train trip (I probably slept), but I do remember being taken to the local parish hall upon arrival at our destination, where the village residents who had volunteered to take in evacuees were waiting to choose their 'foster children for the duration'. I was chosen by the Squire's family, together with another little girl who looked like my twin (we were both fair, with blue eyes and blonde page-boy haircuts). Actually, we hadn't even known each other before being placed side by side on the bench, waiting to be picked. We also had both been dressed in pale green coats and hats, which made us look more alike.

r city children from nes without a ·den, or with a ·ch of grass no ·ger than a pocket ·dkerchief, having ·ole fields on the ·rstep to play in ·s an undreamed-of ·ight.

Above: *A leisurely country ramble.*
Right: *Children from London and Gravesend go tree-climbing in Devon.*

Below: *Those too tiny to tackle the trees had to content themselves with clambering over a stile.*

Left: *Out in the Devon fields, little Ann Cameron (5), Audrey Howe (6) and Marie Gudgeon (6), all from London, listen to a Mickey Mouse story told by their teacher, Betty Hall.*
Below: *Berry-picking in the sunshine.*

The Squire's estate was huge and surrounded by a stone wall with cut glass on the top to discourage trespassers. The house was named 'The Poplars'. The Squire was also the Magistrate for the county of Durham (I later learned). The family consisted of him and his wife (Mr and Mrs Fenwick) and their two unmarried daughters, who were to take charge of us, as Mr and Mrs Fenwick were quite old (or so it seemed to us at the time). The daughters themselves were middle-aged. We were to address them as 'Miss Bessie' and 'Miss Muriel'. They were kind to us, but strict, and we were not allowed to play with the neighbourhood children. We missed our families very much, and I lived for my mother's visits. She worked full time in Newcastle and had to take the bus when she could get time off to come and visit me.

The grounds of the estate were extensive, containing a tennis court, terraced gardens, large trees (poplar, naturally, and other kinds, as well as many fruit trees); also an aviary for breeding budgerigars. They also had cattle and turkeys, chickens and pigs. As well as having their own vegetable garden, they also grew produce on one of the wartime plots (Victory gardens I believe they were called). They had gardeners and domestic staff. I remember they grew corn but they called it Indian maize. We children usually ate with the kitchen staff, apart from the evening meal when we joined the adults.

The house had a beautiful library and I spent countless hours there reading beautifully bound fairy tales. The library had an adjoining conservatory where they grew grapes and peaches.

The family also were one of the only automobile-owners in the village (apart from perhaps the doctor and dentist). It was a two-seater with a rumble seat, and I only saw it out a couple of times, and I only remember being in it once. (Probably because of the petrol shortage.)

Stanhope was a lovely little village surrounded by moors and fells, and I completely fell in love with it and was quite brokenhearted when I had to leave to come home (which was then Newcastle upon Tyne) in 1943, I believe.

I remember the summer fête they'd have, and being dressed up like Little Bo Peep one year, with a real lamb; and another year as a Japanese girl in a real kimono. Unfortunately, I don't remember anyone taking photographs of these events.

I also remember convoys of troops causing much excitement when they'd drive through the village. I even remember the Misses Fenwick entertaining army officers from time to time. Every Sunday we attended the village Church of England with the family and ogled the choirboys (who were mostly boys from the Borstal boys' school). After church we

**PIG
FOOD**

WASTE FOOD
FOR THE FEEDING OF PIGS

Put IN Bin.	Do NOT put in Bin.
Potato and Apple Peelings	Rhubarb or Potato Tops
Pea Shells	Tea Leaves
Scraps of Meat	Coffee Grounds
Waste Bread	Skins of Oranges, Lemons,
Cabbage, Lettuce Leaves	Grape Fruit or Bananas
etc., etc.	Salt, Soap or Soda

PLEASE KEEP AS DRY AS POSSIBLE
AND REPLACE LID OF BIN

Children as well as adults did their bit for the wartime anti-waste campaign: kitchen scraps are salvaged for pig food.

took long walks in the countryside. It was frowned upon to play with a ball or a skipping-rope or anything like that on a Sunday. One had to stay dressed in one's Sunday best (of course, out of sight of the adults, you could always chase each other around the fields and meadows).

The local school was quite small, but I remember the teachers being very nice – I believe some of them had come from the city also. We used to be taken on field trips in the area looking for fossils, and also to gather foxgloves and sphagnum moss for the war effort. I know the foxgloves were for digitalis, but I forget what the moss was for.

I stayed at the Fenwicks' for a couple of years I believe, but my little friend went home after a year or so. I became sick with mumps and was hospitalized at the isolation hospital, because Mrs Fenwick was ailing at the time, and they decided that I should be billeted elsewhere after I came out of hospital as they would not be able to take proper care of me.

My next home was with a childless couple living in the village, and I was then getting to be ten years old and probably a little bit moody and harder to handle. I wasn't too happy with them, but at last I was able to play with the other children and it really was a more normal life. I joined the Brownies and dancing class when I was with them, and I remember writing home to my mother to please send me a 'bally dress' as I was to be in a concert. They had a good laugh at that. The concert was the pantomime *Cinderella*, and I was a fairy in the chorus. The pantomime was staged at the town hall and everyone attended and I remember how thrilled I was to be part of it.

I believe it was the summer of 1943 when my mother came to take me home, and even though it was wonderful to think of being home with her again, I was very sad at leaving Stanhope. At the time I never thought of keeping in touch with anyone by writing to them, so I lost touch altogether. I can still imagine it as it was then. I've never been back to England since emigrating to Canada in 1949, but if I ever do go back, Stanhope will be at the top of my list for visiting, although I'm sure there have been many changes since 1943.

Netta Parks (née Thompson) also has rosy memories of her years as an evacuee:

I was an evacuee from June 2nd, 1940 to July 1943. I went with my school, the Harwich County High School, as a 13-year-old schoolgirl. I shall never forget that bright, sunny Sunday morning when we left Harwich, Essex to arrive in Wotton-under-Edge, Gloucestershire, after a journey which took us all day. The only person on that special train who knew where we were going was our headmaster. Neither our parents nor

left: Pupils from the Harwich County High School in their classroom at Wotton-under-Edge, Gloucestershire. Netta Thompson is sitting in the second row, third from the right.
right: Netta Thompson and her grandmother in Miss Mabel Neal's garden in Wotton-under-edge.

our teachers knew where we were going.

In the early evening our train was met at the station by several buses which took us to our final destination. We were met by the local Town Council, and our prospective foster parents looked us over. My friend and I went together to a large house in the village owned by an old lady who had an absolutely potty maid called Emily and a Dalmatian called Pudding.

The first night we had a rubber sheet on the bed. We thought this was hilarious and it sent us off into fits of laughter. It wasn't until later that we learned that the local people had expected small children – and we were at the ripe old age of 13.

After a few weeks I moved to another house owned by three 'maiden' ladies where I stayed for three years. I visited these dear people during a visit to England in 1973 and kept in touch with them until their deaths.

It was a great adventure for us all, and although sometimes the 'great unknown' was a little frightening, the happy times are the ones you

1943 HARWICH COUNTY HIGH SCHOOL TO BE REOPENED

Evacuated Children A Credit To The Borough

The Harwich County High School are returning, and the school will be reopened on September 29th. This very welcome piece of information was given to the "Standard" this week by Alderman L. . Govenor of . . . when the children left the borough and their homes. Before the child schools . . .

On the blackboard:

8. Does the boy like football?
9. I do not like it?
10. The house has many windows
11. This apple does not seem ripe
12. The ship has left the harbour
13. A bat does not fl...
14. The fairy was very tiny
15. Was the horse killed?
fairies

One of the advantages of being transferred to school in the countryside – lessons in the open air.

remember. I suppose nowadays people would call the terrific difference between living in a coastal town in East Anglia and moving into the middle of the Cotswolds 'culture shock'. We didn't know about things like that back then; we just knew we missed the sea and the beaches, but loved the beautiful woods filled with wild flowers and the hills surrounding them.

Jim Walker was evacuated by train from Belfast:

I don't remember very many tears being shed, as this was going to be a great adventure for us city kids. Well, after a number of hours our group arrived at a church hall outside Portrush and the billeting process began. My chum and I began to feel uneasy, as names were being called and the kids were taken away until he and I were the only 'unclaimed baggage' left – surnames both beginning with 'W'. For a couple of kids away from home more or less for the first time, things were getting scary, especially as people were gathered in a little group speaking quietly and glancing every now and again in our direction.

All of a sudden, one of them marched over to us – she did appear to be a bit of a martinet type – and said that we were to go with her until our billeting was settled. She drove us to a cottage in the middle of nowhere and to our surprise entertained us royally with cookies, candies, etc. It was not long before she got a phone call and we left for our billet, which turned out to be in the delightful little village of Bushmills, and the house we were to stay in had a good view of the Old Bush distillery, which did not mean as much to me then (eleven years old) as it does now.

I must say that Mrs McEachern and her sister, both ex-Scotland, could not have treated us better. It was a beautiful house, with the River Bush flowing past their back garden.

The village kids and the 'vacees' got on really well and we had our own 'test matches' and soccer games. The shopkeepers felt sorry for these 'wee waifs' away from home and sold us chocolate and broken biscuits at half price, so we had no trouble making buddies with the village kids. My best friend's father was the newsagent, so I got to read all the comics, *Hotspur* etc., before they went on sale.

Being city kids we made many a goof, the big one being the first week after we arrived. About six of us were walking along one of the roads when we spotted an orchard, and in true city fashion climbed over the wall and started to fill our pockets with fruit. All of a sudden this huge dog appeared with some man waving a stick. Well, we all got away; however, as the saying goes, 'Your sins will find you out.' On Sunday morning we were all whisked off to the local Presbyterian church to Sunday

School, and guess what – the minister was the man who had waved his stick at us. From then on we only had to go up to his door to get an apple or two. But imagine our embarrassment!

Joan Keane (now Wood) found she was readily accepted and well looked after by her foster families:

I was evacuated in 1939. I was almost 14, so probably remember more than the younger children.

I lived in Irlam, near Manchester, and attended Adelphi House School, a convent grammar school in Salford. On September 2nd 1939 many of us were evacuated to Accrington, Lancashire.

We had luggage-labels fastened to our coats and carried our gas-masks and small bags or cases holding a few essential items of clothing. We went by train and on arrival were taken to a centre where volunteers were trying to sort us out and find suitable foster homes for us. Some people came to the centre and chose children who took their fancy. The rest of us were 'hawked' round the neighbourhood, knocking on doors and asking people to take us in. It didn't seem to be very well organized, but I suppose it had been sprung on them at fairly short notice. Some poor kids were still there late at night waiting for someone to take pity on them and give them a home.

We were each given a carrier bag containing some items of food. I remember there was a tin of corned beef, evaporated milk and a block of York plain chocolate. There was probably sugar and tea, but I can't remember exactly what else it contained.

Being little convent girls, we were all moderately bright, clean, respectable and well behaved, so were fairly soon accepted, but there were cases of not very attractive children being rejected, and other stories of the appalling habits and behaviour of some of them. Fortunately there were some kindly souls who were prepared to accept them – warts and all. One large homely lady turned up at one reception centre and said, 'Give me the two scruffiest little buggers you can find and I'll take 'em home and bath 'em.'

Another girl from my class and I were billeted with a family who had volunteered to take one boy. They had intended to let him sleep in the same room as the wife's old father, so it meant some reorganization of beds and bedding arrangements to accommodate us. They had never had any children of their own, but were very kind. The other girl and I had never really been friends at school, but we got on well together and are still in touch after all these years though we are both now in our 60s.

A few days later, my friend's mother visited us and was convinced that

Joan Keane (right) with the girl who was billeted with her, Mary Nield, and their foster parents' grandson, Geoffrey Bridge, in Accrington, September 1939.

*Children evacuated to
Liskeard, Cornwall go
out shopping with Mrs
Pickard.*

the woman had TB, so she insisted on getting us rebilleted. I didn't really want to go and remember crying bitterly for hours. I suppose it was pent-up emotion of the whole traumatic experience. However, she found us another billet with two middle-aged, lovely kind people who hadn't expected to have evacuees at all. The woman was in her mid-50s and had a grown-up son who was married and had a little boy called Geoffrey, about three years old, who used to visit regularly. We loved him. The son and his wife were both music teachers and we used to have tea with them quite often. We were taken to visit many of their friends, too, and were always accepted quite naturally.

They were ordinary working-class people with simple tastes and few luxuries, but not short of essentials. The house was a terraced, two-up, two-down type with an outside 'loo', but it was clean and cosy and we

Sixty-seven-year-old Mrs Annie Norris, who was awarded the British Empire Medal for her devotion in caring for six evacuees, serves her charges breakfast.

al-times were quite
occasion for Mrs
dge of Birdham,
r Chichester and
houseful of
cuees.

were well looked after. 'Aunt Hannah', as we were told to call her, did all our washing and fed us as well as possible on good plain home cooking. 'Uncle Tom' worked in a local cotton mill and used to leave early in the morning. They were Protestants and he was a Freemason, but our foster mum used to waken us in time to go to mass every morning, and had our breakfast ready for us on our return. For this I think she received ten shillings a week for each of us, and our parents had to pay the authority seven shillings a week.

By Christmas 1939 so many children had returned home that they decided to let the rest do the same. Air raids hadn't started, so the panic was over. They called it the 'phoney' war. Other schools elsewhere persevered longer.

Right: *An outdoor milk-and-medicine session.*
Below: *Boys from the evacuated Mill Hill School in North London dine in what was once a dance hall at the Seacote Hotel in St Bees, Cumberland.*

Thirsty work, all this fresh air and country living . . .

We shared a local convent school, going in half-days, alternating mornings one week, afternoons the next. We never met the other girls, but used to leave notes for each other in the desks. Our staff used to spend a few days with us and a few days back at our school in Salford teaching the children who had stayed at home. When we were all back home, life returned to 'normal' in spite of air raids, bombs, broken windows and the other disruptions. One of our nuns was killed by a bomb which damaged the convent chapel.

For the young Walker brothers Cyril and Ivor, from Manchester, evacuation 'held no fears at all':

In fact we were quite excited venturing into the 'unknown', which turned out to be a middle-class suburb some six miles away called Timperley.

With Dad away in the Navy, Mum bade us a brave goodbye on Saturday September 2nd, 1939. As most of our pals from the local school were with us, it was quite a happy occasion, enjoying our first railway journey on the electric train. At Timperley School we were soon allocated to a nice young couple who took us home to their 'posh' house: garden, inside toilet, hot water, electricity – a new world!

On Sunday September 3rd we were allowed out to play and to explore our new neighbourhood. The canal was close by a natural habitat, so, oblivious of time or distance, our young healthy legs took us unwittingly towards Manchester. At Chester Road, Old Trafford, I said to my brother, 'Blimey, we're nearly home . . . might as well call in home for a drink of water.' Twenty minutes later we strolled through the front door as if we had just come from school.

Mother was completely shocked into silence, her face showing horrors of a million possibilities. Her eventual outcry is unprintable; suffice to say that our innocent explanation was never considered and we were frogmarched to Old Trafford station and bundled aboard the next train.

At Timperley our guardian asked anxiously, 'Where have you two been?' 'Only walking around,' was the innocent reply – well, we were!

Many of the children were homesick and begged their parents to come and take them back home. Mary Humphries (now McCallum) stayed away for just a few short weeks:

I was evacuated with my sister, and almost every other child in the town I think, the day before war broke out. We lived in Gosport, Hampshire, and they assumed (as it turned out, quite rightly) that it was a prime target for bombing by the Germans, being on the east side of Portsmouth

*cuees from
dington try their
d at digging the
len on the Oxley
estate.*

harbour with all the naval shipping, submarine base, naval bases etc. Gosport and the surrounding area was also home to Army barracks, Marine barracks, Royal Naval Air Station, RAF Station etc. They could hardly miss hitting something.

We were all put on trains, with large labels pinned on to our clothes with our names and addresses. Each of us was given a brown carrier bag filled with groceries, which included cans of evaporated milk (which we were served diluted and heated before going to bed each night until it ran out). We had no idea where we were going, but ended up in Eastleigh, Hampshire. We were all assembled in a local school and the local people chose who they would billet. My sister and I and two other girls ended up in a lovely house with large grounds – they had a Swiss maid, which impressed us no end. They really wanted four boys to stay with them to help out with the gardening, because their gardeners had been called up for military service, so they weren't too thrilled to end up with four girls aged between nine and twelve years. However, they were very kind and gave us great accommodation. After a week or so we started going to school

*Farmers of the future
City schoolboys learn
how to make hay and
plough a furrow.*

All part of the war effort: helping to bring home the bacon in a time when meat was scarce and strictly rationed.

half-days, the local children going the other half-day.

After a few weeks, during which time I had my eleventh birthday, we were so homesick and missed our parents so much that we begged and pleaded with our parents to let us return, which we did after about six weeks. The other two girls stayed on. All the schools had been closed for lack of students when we returned, but after a while some parents allowed small groups of children and a teacher to use a room in their home each morning. We didn't get too much education that year, but we were happy to be back home. Eventually enough children returned, schools were opened again – and of course the bombing started. But that's another story.

I'm glad we did return, because my father was knocked down and killed in the black-out in 1943, and at least we were all together for the last years of his life.

Temporarily reunited for Christmas, parents and children greet each other with unsuppressed joy at Nottingham station.

*reen Milton (left)
side her
ndmother's house
Rhoscolyn, with her
ther, her sister,
drey, and the dog,
ss.*

Doreen Milton (now Berning) first witnessed evacuation from the receiving end, at her grandmother's house, and then became an evacuee herself:

My grandmother lived in Rhoscolyn on Holy Island off Anglesey, and with my parents and my sister we used to visit her every holiday time. My grandmother had a large detached house (rented not owned) in the middle of a field and used to take in holidaymakers. In a corner of the field was a chalet which we, and other members of the family, used to use when Grandma's house was full of guests. We were in Anglesey when war was declared. Dad returned to Salford as he was on the 'reserve list', having been in the Army in the other war, and Mum, my sister and I stayed behind with Bess (our dog).

After only a few days, word arrived that the people in Rhoscolyn were to take in evacuees from Liverpool, and we went to the local school to await their arrival. Grandma finished up with quite a large family, I can't remember exactly how many, but I think it was about six. They must have been very poor (we weren't exactly affluent), as when they were taken to bed their first words were, 'Can we get in between the sheets?'

Many were the baths they needed to get them clean – and this necessitated heating the water collected in the rain-water butt – but our days in Anglesey ended when Mum decided that we should return to join Dad, and that my sister and I should join the band of evacuees in order to carry on with our education.

The rest of our schoolfriends had already been found accommodation when my sister and I arrived in Accrington (incidentally, the first place in the North to receive the attentions of Hitler in the form of a bomb on the brickworks). I think we must have followed about two weeks after the first batch. As far as I remember, about eight of us arrived in the reception centre and were then hawked around the area to find anyone willing to take us in. We eventually were taken in by a family called Butterworth. I was then thirteen and my sister was ten.

Schooling was shared. The local schools had the morning or afternoon, and we took the other period alternately. We put on a show for our hosts, and I can remember it vividly. Our school (show-offs) put on a play all in French about the children of the French Revolution. I can still remember one of my lines, which went, 'Mais madame, les jeunes demoiselles portent des jolies pantoufles; si on les remarque dans la rue, on se doute d'elles.' Loosely translated, it meant, 'But madam, the young ladies are wearing pretty shoes and if they are noticed in the street they will cause suspicion.'

We also combined all the cast to sing songs to well-known tunes. To

Doreen Milton (centre) with her mother and sister in Rhoscolyn, just above the beach known as Lily Pond Bay.

the tune of the *Merry Widow* waltz went:

Every night my wife's relations called in for bridge,
Played a bit and then they guzzled eats from the fridge,
When I forgot the sporting two they soon discarded me,
My wife said, 'Henry clear out do, and join the ARP.'

By Christmas time we were back with our parents (we had been coming home every other weekend anyway).

Valerie Gibbs (the late Valerie Benest) ended up in the village of Lacock, near Bath:

I and another girl, Margaret Thompson, were taken in by a kindly old lady, Gertrude Hayden, who lived with her stepfather, John Chivers, in an old thatched worker's cottage which was on the Doel family farm.

It was late afternoon when we eventually got settled in, given a small bedroom on the upper level, both sharing a double bed. Margaret later returned home and I was left by myself with Mrs Hayden for the next two years.

I can remember on my first day sitting on a stile at the end of the garden looking out across the fields and thinking how quiet it was after London and wondering if I would ever see my parents again.

The days developed into a routine, getting up at sunrise; old John Chivers left early to do the milking on the Doel farm. After breakfast we walked the 1½ miles to the old abbey where we attended school, there being no room at the village school for the London kids. The abbey was owned by the Talbot family and was the site where Henry Fox Talbot conducted his many early photographic experiments resulting in the invention of the negative/positive process. The abbey was later given to the

Mrs Muriel Duncan of Knoll House, Uppingham, Rutlandshire inaugurated the first home for children under the age of five who were evacuated without their mothers. Here, they receive Christmas presents from their 'nanny'.

Christmas was a time when many evacuees missed their families more than ever, but foster parents and teachers did their best to make the children feel at home. This little trio is pictured at a school party in Shenfield, Essex.

Valerie Gibbs pictured, above, outside her foster home in Lacock, Wiltshire and, right, with her foster mother, Mrs Hayden, 1942.

National Trust in 1944.

Classes were held in one of the passageways in the old abbey. The age of the old abbey gave it a mystery and raised all kinds of scary thoughts in the minds of the kids. Going to the 'lav' was particularly scary; it was situated in the crypt below the abbey.

My mum and dad used to visit when they could and always left for home loaded with fresh vegetables. I was always sent up to the farm to ask the farmer's son to shoot some rabbits for my mum and dad.

Other memories include cow-plop-hopping, with the resulting messy shoes when the crust wasn't hard enough, and collecting wild flowers – violets, primroses, cowslips and bluebells. These fond memories still remain, resulting in my love of wild flowers to this day. Haymaking, threshing, mushrooming and nut-collecting all became the natural order of living. I grew to know where all the best spots were – and I mustn't forget blackberrying time.

I remember the visits to the local pedlars; paraffin, candles etc., also Wiltshire pies, sausages, black pudding and Bath chops from the bacon factory in Calne. The bus to Bath came only once a week; a local bus to Chippenham or Melksham ran once a day, but a bus trip was a rare event for us kids.

I also have fond memories of the soft, lilting Wiltshire accent that can be found even today.

Film shows were held in the village hall each Friday evening. My favourite was *Felix the Cat*. Hard wooden benches were set out and were quickly filled; if there was no room you sat on the floor.

By early 1942 I was back in London. The 'Battle of Britain' was over, and my dad had been called into the Army and wanted me to be with my mother.

Lacock had become part of me, and later, when any opportunity presented itself I would take the trip back home to Auntie Hayden.

Marjorie Williams (now Hole) found a wonderful four-legged friend in her foster home:

My Auntie Bess and Uncle Joe, I can't remember too much about them, but they had a gorgeous dog called Lady and she really took to me. She used to go to the school gates with me, go home, and be waiting for me coming out. Anyway, it was proper winter in Colne, near Nelson in Lancashire – thick snow. We all had to wear cloaks, and Uncle Joe made me a proper sledge; I used to put my gas-mask on it, I hated carrying it. Lady liked to sit on the sledge with me.

I will always remember how I didn't let the war bother me. We never saw any action or doodlebugs or anything. Anyway, I was to have adventures.

I went to the beck [stream] with Lady, and all the ice was melting. The river was full, flowing very fast, and then it happened – the dog got through the railings and down the steep slope to the beck and into it. She seemed to be struggling, so I went down to save her, but I couldn't get back. There was a twig sticking out; I clung on because the water was going that fast it was pushing me over, and I was screaming; I thought I was going to drown.

Lady was barking all round me. Anyway, someone shouted, 'Hang on, love!' but the twig was snapping, and then I saw a fellow walking and struggling towards me. He was big, he picked me up in his arms and into an ambulance.

They kept me for the night. I couldn't stop shivering and I wouldn't shut up. I wanted to know where Lady was, was told she was all right, and the nurse said, 'Go to sleep.'

Well, when I went back to the old couple they said I was always up to something and it was upsetting, and I would have to go. I cried, 'I love you all!' I didn't want ever to leave the dog, and I was under the table when they came for me. I clung to the dog, the dog's eyes were wet and she was yelping. I kissed Bess and Joe; then they found me a new place.

Left: *Two little girls with buckets and spades survey the beach through a barrier of barbed wire, 1940.*
Below: *Stripped to the bare seaside essentials – bathing suit and gas-mask.*

Reginald Slee went to the beautiful countryside of South West England:

The destination station we arrived at was or is called Fraddon, which is near St Columb Road and Indian Queens, Cornwall. Today the journey by train [from London] only takes about four to five hours. Fraddon Road station lies about seven miles from the seaside resort of Newquay, which is known as the Cornish Riviera. I have been there quite a few times in my adult life, and when I am travelling down by car it brings back a lot of memories.

When all the children, including myself, and the teachers who were in charge of the evacuee party had got off the train, the teachers assembled us all together in two lines ready to walk to the school hall, which was about ten or twelve minutes' walk from the station. Having arrived at the school hall, we had to wait while the authorities in charge went to the people's houses in Indian Queens and surrounding villages, asking them how many evacuees each house could or would take. Some took one, some took two, others took more.

I was billeted with a married couple who had no children of their own, with another evacuee. The couple were aged about forty to forty-five. It was about half-past seven to eight o'clock when we arrived at their house, which was a semi-detached house about a hundred yards from the school in the same road (St Columb Road). We had a wash, a meal and then went to bed; we were very tired. My two sisters were found billets in the same road about two hundred yards from my billet.

The woman's husband where I was billeted was a farm labourer or worked in the china-clay pits, as far as I can remember. He used to go out in the morning on his bicycle, with his shoulder-bag packed with vacuum flask and lunch box, and come back in the late afternoon, when we would have an evening meal. I cannot remember their name, or the name of the other evacuee. They were church people, and we went to the local Methodist church twice on Sundays, morning and evening service.

During my spare time and on Saturdays I used to go to a smallholding that had a few cows and chickens etc. I used to help as best as I could with the milking; it was all done by hand at that time. The smallholding was situated on the main London to Penzance road, the A30. There were also two or three other smallholdings, but they are gone now. I got a bit homesick, and was going to hitch-hike back to London, but there was not much lorry traffic about – though there was plenty of horse-drawn and pony-and-trap traffic – so I had to abandon the idea. We used to go to the china-clay pits to play. My billet parent forbade me to go and play at the pits because it was dangerous, as they used to use explosives to get the

china clay out. I used to lie to him, tell him I had been somewhere else. He got to dislike me and reported me to the authorities, who transferred me to another billet.

I was with the first couple for about three weeks to a month. I got my case packed and my gas-mask, which was in a brownish square box, and I was taken to a new billet about two miles away at a village called Trevarren, which is on the road to St Columb Major. At this new billet, which was owned by an elderly lady – she looked in her sixties – were already six evacuees; I made the seventh.

She had a daughter, aged about forty, who also had two evacuees living with her. Her husband was in the forces somewhere doing his bit for the country. I did not see or hear of the woman's husband I was billeted with. Whether he was in the forces or he'd passed on I don't know.

She was a very strict woman, a real dragon. I suppose she's passed on now. She was very active for her age, always on the go with the house-work and the cooking etc. She used to do all her own cooking, making cakes, plain and seedy buns and Cornish pasties, which were very tasty, made of meat, onions, potatoes and swedes.

For the girls of Mitcham Lane School, Streatham, now evacuated to Llangadog, Carmarthenshire, domestic science escapes the confines of the kitchen . . .

*. while the boys
ush up their
bbling skills in an
en-air boot-
bairing class.*

The other boys were younger than me. We used to have a chore to do – get the water from a pump, or dig a hole in the garden to empty the toilet bucket. The toilets were outside; they were not flush ones then. There was no electricity laid on, so she had to use oil-lamps when it was night-time.

When it was bath night, the younger boys used to bath first, have a bun and a cup of cocoa and then go straight to bed. Bath-time used to start about seven-thirty in the evening; by the time everyone was bathed it was nine o'clock. We were always in bed early, and we used to talk to one another. If the lady heard us she would call out to us, threatening to smack us.

The billet where I was staying was almost on top of a hill. There was a general grocery store and post office next door. I used to get some sweets and a bit of fruit, lemonade, writing paper and stamps with the little money I had at the time, which was not very much. The billet lady was a sort of religious type, who used to make us go to chapel on Sundays, which was over the top of the hill.

The boys at that time always used to wear short trousers till they started work. I used to walk the two miles to school and stop there all day. In the summer-time we used to have our lessons in a field opposite the school. The classes used to consist of about forty pupils.

Opposite where we lived there was a lane, and along this lane there was a dairy farm named Bazeley's, which had a few acres of land, about thirty cows – it may have been more, because Mr Bazeley used to deliver milk locally – and chickens etc. I used to go and help Mr Bazeley to cut the long grass and bracken in the fields. The chickens used to lay their eggs in the bracken and I would gather them up for him. I would cut the grass with a short-handled scythe. He gave me two or three shillings for my work. They used to milk their cows by hand. I never used to help them do that, I just watched them milk and separate the milk. It used to be tuberculosis-tested. Down the bottom of the hill, on the same side as Bazeley's farm, there was a clearing that was called the Kelliards, where I and the other evacuees used to go and play. There were swamps in the clearing, and a river running through it. I used to get a pole, or make one out of a tree branch, and jump across the river and back with the aid of the pole.

Bazeley's farm is not there any more. I don't know if he sold it or passed away. The last time I was that way I saw that some bungalows have been built on the land.

At the time I was evacuated there was an airfield built at a place called St Ivel, two or three miles from St Columb Major. The lorries taking the ballast for the runway used to pass our billet, and I used to get a ride out there and back. Another thing I used to see was that if someone passed away, the undertaker used to wheel the coffin on a type of barrow, with the mourners following behind.

Doreen Chambers (née Crees), who as a child lived in Downham, Kent, recalls her life as an evacuee as 'definitely a happy time':

I can remember the day as though it was yesterday. We were marched from our school – Pendragon Road School, Downham – to Grove Park station, and there lined up on the platform waiting for the train that was to whisk us away to an unknown destination. We were all given postcards to write home when we arrived, and my mother had addressed them home for us all. We were very poor and didn't have suitcases etc; we had pillowcases, each with a tag tied around our necks. We didn't have gas-masks at that point in time, and we went to – would you believe the irony – Folkestone.

Another girl and I were billeted with this really elderly couple, and my brothers were put in another home. I remember on 3rd September,

...ndon children get
... to something fishy
... a village stream.

when the war was actually declared, walking on the beach in Folkestone with the son of the folks we were staying with. I just remember my mother panicking when she heard that we were so close to the French border, coming down on a bus and whipping the three of us up and taking us home again.

Then the next year, 1940, the war was getting into swing and so we were evacuated once again on a train; this time it seemed a dog's age. We arrived at a place called Chard, in Somerset, and we were all sitting cross-legged in a hall being given a sandwich and milk to drink, which really was a luxury for us (having lived all our lives on condensed milk). Then we were separated into groups and allocated to different villages and towns in Somerset. I insisted this time that my mother had told me to stay with my brothers and look after them.

We arrived at a village called Lopen, a very tiny village that only had two classrooms – so you can imagine the catastrophe of having 32 London children literally forced on them. If folks had room to spare, they had to take a child or children.

We were in the church hall and being picked out by all these folks who kept looking us over back and front, I might say. I can remember clinging to my brothers and saying we were not going to be separated, but they finally came down to the fact that one woman wanted two boys and this other dear little old lady (who I thought looked like a witch) was there to pick out a girl for her sister. She kept saying she wanted a little girl younger than I was, but anyway she did after all decide that maybe I would do, and that it would be fine because I could see my brothers' house (where they would be staying) from my bedroom window.

I just couldn't understand their accents; little did I know that two years later I would be talking exactly the same. I must admit that I really did not have the portions to eat that I can remember wanting. My mother sent food parcels the whole time, and kept me nicely clothed, but the woman who looked after me just drew three shillings and sixpence a week for looking after me, and even then that wasn't much to feed a growing girl on.

Although I really missed my family, my mother came down regularly on special buses that were run from our area at home to see us. Then my brother, who was six at the time, wet the bed, so they sent him to another home in Yeovil. My mother came down and took him home, and so just my younger brother and I were left down there.

We had a wonderful teacher from home who was in charge of us; her name was Mrs Norman and she lived in Brockley. She was another mother to us all; we could tell her anything, and she would listen to us crying from time to time, homesick. Our life was spent in these two class-

cuated children go
dling in a stream
uckinghamshire –
the ubiquitous
masks.

rooms, and basically we only learned to read and write and to collect hips and haws from the wild rose-bushes that lined the hedges. The Red Cross collected them to make jam, and we knitted socks for the soldiers.

It was a wonderful experience for us in that we would never have experienced the country, and the local farmer near our house would name calves after us evacuees.

Thousands of remarkable people took in the little strangers and treated them as if they were their own. One look at the sad faces of the children far from home was often all it took to melt their hearts. But it was not always easy or straightforward, as Frances May Guy (now Driscoll) and her husband discovered:

We had the most traumatic experience with evacuated children, which taught us the strength of love (if that is what one would call it) of things they knew, parents, friends or environment.

In January 1940 we were told, not asked, to take in four children from London (one family), the eldest about 12 years, a girl with a face like granite, who bossed the others without a word. The younger ones never took their eyes off her.

My husband and myself were not keen, or willing, as we did not understand children, but we had staying with us a very serious and kind young man who adored children, so we all got stuck in, as it was supposed only to be for two weeks. We fed them, washed them, and decked them out in what clothes we could rake up. We prepared a room with two double beds, gave them sweets and water, and left them to sort out their own sleeping places.

When we thought they must be asleep, our friend went up to check, and came downstairs, three at a time, and white-faced, as there was no sign of them. We looked in every other room, with no result. We rang the billeting people and the police. They looked in the room, and searched the house. Finally, back to the room. They found them when they saw a movement underneath the beds. We were all heartbroken, and had a hard job getting them *into* the beds. The police doctor gave them some tablets and we watched them until they slept, and our friend put a mattress on the floor for himself.

No amount of coaxing would make them settle, so finally they had to be sent home, as all they wanted was Mum and Dad and the 'safety' of the slum – but *home* – they knew. Even the nice clothes we scrounged for them got no reaction, and the money they were given was taken, like they would take bus fare or dinner money.

They left us just yearning to know what happened to the rock-faced little wonder. It was a case of 'ships that pass in the night', but it taught us to study children and realize that if the going is tough enough, kids can be as logical as adults, even more so.

P.S. We took no more evacuees, as we were ourselves bombed out, three weeks later.

Monica Cromack (now Hale) lived in Leatherhead, Surrey, where her mother was one of those who took evacuated children into their homes:

We had an evacuee from Streatham [London]. Her name was Gwenny, and her dad was a detective at Scotland Yard. She was a cheerful soul, but her mother missed her terribly. Every Friday after school we took Gwenny to Leatherhead railway station. Her mother would arrive on the train from Streatham, cross under the tracks over to the London side, have a tearful reunion, and whisk Gwenny off back to Streatham for the weekend. I remember when we saw them off before Christmas, the mother gave my mother a bottle of port!

It was awful for the evacuees and their parents: on Sundays we would see them wandering round the town together, with only the Crescent cinema and some little cafés to go to if it was wet – which it usually was.

*Home-made
entertainment at an
evacuees' party at St
Peter's Hall, Brighton.*

Marion Pikes (now Lister) lived near Hereford in a village called Withington, which became the temporary home of evacuees from a number of regions:

When war broke out in September 1939, practically a whole school from Birmingham was evacuated to the village. It was Osler Street School, and we had several teachers as well as children. They were billeted with people who had room for them. Of course nothing much happened in those early days, so that by Christmas most of them had returned home to Birmingham. They didn't like village life – 'too far between bus stops' and 'no life' and also 'so dark'! (But surely it would have been dark in Birmingham with the black-outs?)

In September 1940 we had Londoners from Mile End Road [in East London]. My mother and I put up five of them for quite a time; we were allowed 18 shillings a week for a grown-up and five shillings a week for a child. They ate all our home-made jam and thought village life was very boring – 'What do you *do*?'

Later on during the war, a battery of soldiers took over a very large empty house, and from time to time their wives would come to the village for a week or so. They often came from cities that had been bombed, and enjoyed the peace and did much to liven up the community. We had village concerts and dances regularly.

During these times the village school was filled to bursting-point with city children. I was a teacher, and we had classes in the village hall and 'managed' with using whist tables instead of desks, and sharing one blackboard and easel. For one short period I had a class of 57 infants, a number of whom were Geordies. We spoke different languages, but we were all happy.

I was Honorary Secretary of the Red Cross Agriculture Fund, and cycled for miles collecting pennies per week from various places. We organized whist drives, jumble sales, dances and social evenings, and money raised went to the Red Cross fund or to the SSAFA [Soldiers', Sailors' and Airmen's Families Association], or to the Merchant Navy, although we were so far from the sea.

As a ten-year-old boy, John Hoodless, who lived in Cargo, near the Scottish border, watched as evacuees arrived in his village in September 1939:

We had around 40 mixed evacuees sent across from the Newcastle area. This almost doubled the numbers in the village school, which took children from the ages of five to 14 years old, mixed. We had two teachers, a

For many city children there was more to learn in the countryside than just arithmetic!

Miss Thompson, who took the infants up to eight years old, and the headmaster, a Mr Musgrave, who took the remainder. When the evacuees arrived we were given two weeks' extra holiday until everything was sorted out.

The 'Geordies' brought two teachers with them, a Miss Veitch and a man teacher, I can't remember his name. The children were spread into various houses in the village, and I remember three brothers, one aged five, one nine and one 13, were all in the same house, the biggest house in the village, owned by two bachelor brothers. I remember the youngest of these three brothers had a glass eyes, and the party piece was that one of the brothers would hold him by his feet and shake him until his eye dropped out.

Theresa Wood (now Backhouse) was evacuated from Armley, Leeds, with her brother and sister. Her education definitely suffered as a result – temporarily, at least:

We lived in Armley at the time and attended the Holy Family School. We were evacuated to Louth in Lincolnshire. I still have a photo of the Old

Mill, where we stayed, that my sister sent my mother. On the reverse side it says:

Dear Mother and Daddy,
We start school on Monday. We go in the afternoon. The picture at the back is where we are staying. We have got a lot of toys. Love Rita and xxxxxxx

The second card was sent from me, but the housekeeper wrote it as I was only six (Rita was nine):

Hubbard's Hill Louth.

Dear Mother and Daddy,
We are having a nice time. We have been all round the hill which is at the back of the picture & have fed the swans. I'm a good girl. We are going to church tomorrow for the first time. Start school Monday afternoon. xxxxxxxxxxxxx

Our 'host' was a lovely country gentleman called Mr Parker. However, after Mr Parker had gathered us into his arms, a woman in that drab, old hall said that she wanted an evacuee and against Mr Parker's wishes insisted on her rights. She separated my dear sister from us, and Rita had the most awful time. The woman had some very young children, and Rita was made to do the shopping and washing and was, in general, a skivvy.

My Irish grandmother found out about this, and she and my mother travelled to Louth to have her removed. Mr Parker was still keen to keep the family together.

When they arrived at the council offices, they were met with a good deal of red tape, and in a nutshell were told that Rita could not be moved, whereupon my mother cried; but my fiery grandmother said she would not leave the building till she had seen the Lord Mayor himself! (One of the first sit-ins?) She attacked the Lord Mayor verbally when he arrived until she had got her way, and Rita came to us at the Old Mill.

We did go to school on that first Monday, as planned, but there was no bus to take us home and we walked three miles back to the Old Mill. It was very dark and frightening walking back, as it was pitch black because of the black-out, and being in the country too didn't help. Mr Parker said that if there wasn't a bus we wouldn't go to school. There wasn't!

Mr Parker's house was big and old. There was a huge dog called Bonzo who was so big I could ride on his back. We all loved him.

Every week the children from a nearby primary school came to play in the grounds of the Old Mill. There were some roughly made swings, and Mr Parker had a rope hanging from a fairly high branch and used to say that there was sixpence at the top if anyone climbed up. The children from the school treated us with disdain. They wouldn't speak to us – they had perhaps been warned about 'city' children. All, that is, except one boy called Danny, who was a bit of a tearaway. The only boy to ever climb the rope! My sister spent some time in hospital with diphtheria when we were there, and both Michael and I were germ-carriers. Perhaps this is another reason why we didn't go to school.

I'm not sure how long we were in Louth. My mother, now 84, is very vague, but she thinks it was about a year. I know that when we eventually did come back and go back to school, I could neither read nor write. I was at the bottom of the class and definitely regarded as stupid by my teacher, Miss Clark. I hated school for this reason. It was many years before I recovered from the traumatic return after the peaceful countrified life we'd led – shades of Thomas Hardy!

I failed my 11-plus and at 15 went to work in a factory, cutting out dresses. I was a dress designer at 23. I married and went to West Africa for seven years. My husband taught classics. I started teaching at a small private school. When we returned, and four children later, I did a teacher-training course myself. I now teach French in a middle school. I did a degree in French a few years ago – so all's well that ends well!

Sally Koldinsky (now Waldes), who was evacuated from Hackney, in London's East End, was plunged into an environment she was totally unaccustomed to:

My father was injured during a troops landing in France and was brought back to England and hospitalized. It was at this point that my brother and I were evacuated so that my mother could travel to Newcastle to stay with my father. We were tagged and labelled and bombarded with safety instructions, and I remember hundreds of children standing with us on the platform of the station ready to face the unknown haven of Sheffield. My specific instructions were not to let go of my brother's hand for any reason. I was almost 11 and Mel, my brother, was six years younger, so this was a great responsibility for me which I did not take lightly.

During that unhappy journey my brother was taken ill with severe stomach cramps and had to be taken off the train – but I'd been specifically told not to let go of his hand! Of course, I was not allowed to go with him and had to remain on the train. What would my mother say? I had abandoned him to strangers and didn't know whether I would ever see him again.

My next recollection is of sitting with all the kids in a school and waiting for these strange people to claim us. Unfortunately, I was not claimed that day and, alone, spent the night in an air-raid shelter with no blanket or pillow, feeling very bewildered and scared. However, the following morning someone told me to come back into the school, which seemed so desolate and quiet, and, lo and behold, there was a man in a dark blue uniform and peaked cap waiting to take me somewhere. As I learned later, this person was the chauffeur to the family I was lucky enough to be boarded with. Little Sally from Hackney was to experience the unknown world of luxury. Mr and Mrs Cussins, the family I stayed with, had one daughter, Audrey, who was away at boarding school, but I was told that she was the same age as me. I was given her bedroom and the use of all the many wonderful toys and games; there was even a sink in the bedroom and a telephone. I had never been that close to a telephone before, nor had I ever seen a sink in a bedroom. This was just another beautiful room in a fairy-tale mansion.

On the first night there I remember being called down to dinner by the maid, Sarah. On my descent, there appeared to be many magnificently dressed people in long gowns, and the men in evening dress, holding their glasses in a toast to the poor little evacuee (apparently I was something of a novelty to these people, who had never seen a cockney child). This was all too much for me, and all I could do was sob my heart out and call for my mum. My next impression was of awe – being led into a huge dining room of mirrors and shining silver platters, where the table was laden with sumptuous-looking food. However, all I could think about was my little brother. I was later told that he was fine and living with a family not too far from where I was. I begged to see him and eventually did so a few days later. He was very sad and lonely and complained of being hungry. I discovered he was staying with an equally well-to-do family in the steel industry, but they did not believe in big portions and were very strict with him. In the days that followed, one of my chief goals was to supply Mel with food sneaked out of my house, and I would meet him after school with my little package of food.

I was enrolled at the local school, of which I remember nothing. I do remember many rides with the chauffeur in a huge limousine and my introduction by him to the wonderful world of nature of which I was totally ignorant. He showed me fields of primroses, the first I had ever seen, and we visited farms and were shown the animals, quite foreign to a city girl, and the friendly farmers gave us eggs for the missus.

There was also a very nice lady who lived in an even bigger mansion on my street, who introduced me to the world of reading in her huge library, a massive room where all the walls were covered by books. I do believe this is where my passion for reading and classical music started, as I

*Right: Mrs Randolph Churchill lent her home, Eichelfond House, in Hertfordshire, for use as a war nursery. Here, the matron and two of the nurses take the children for a walk in the grounds.
Below: Evacuees in Rye, Kent explore their new neighbourhood with a local old-timer.*

would sit in that room for hours at a time with some gentle prodding to read certain books and listen to the music. Most of the time I spent with adults, because the neighbourhood children were at boarding schools.

My eleventh birthday was celebrated with Mr and Mrs Cussins who made a big party for me with a birthday cake and presents. I don't know where all the children came from or who they were, but they were all dressed so nicely and this was my very first birthday party. Why then was I so unhappy? Amid all the luxury and attention I was very lonely and homesick for my mum, the old flat and cramped bedroom I shared with my older sister and little brother.

In every fairy story there is always a witch and my one was Sarah, the maid. I believe she resented my good fortune, and whenever possible she would treat me badly, although I cannot remember the details. All I can remember of Sarah was her sneakiness and the chores she gave me to do – one of them being cleaning a mountain of silver every Friday while she disappeared. I grew to detest this job, and to this day, whenever I clean my own silver – which is not very often – a cloud appears on the horizon!

Mr and Mrs Cussins, the kind people I stayed with, were mystified and awestruck by my being able to take care of myself. Naturally, their daughter had always been pampered and had never had to do anything for herself. So a great deal of excitement ensued when it was found that my hankies, socks and knickers were washed every night by me, in my own lovely sink. I couldn't understand what all the fuss was about.

After several weeks had passed, I was still no happier, but apparently Mr and Mrs Cussins decided that here was a little girl who would make an ideal sister for Audrey, their only child. They contacted my mother, by letter I presume, and paid the train fare to Sheffield and arranged for her and my sister Helen to stay with their friends for a couple of days. An afternoon tea party was arranged, with lots of people, and there were trays of little sandwiches and dainty cakes. I remember snatches of conversation about holidays in the South of France, the Riviera and other exotic-sounding places.

My poor mother sat there dumbstruck like an alien from another planet. I learned later that this was all done to give my mother a good impression of the kind of life I would have if she were to give me up and allow them to adopt me. The proposition was that I would be given the opportunity of living in a good home, have the best education and a career in the family business (a large furniture company) and the chance for a good life. My mother realized what they were offering and knew that she and my father could never provide me with this kind of life but, of course, did not want to give me away.

So the final decision was mine to make and, needless to say, I chose to

*...art class al fresco.
...r children who were
...ed to the scenery of
...ban skylines,
...ndscape-painting in
...e country was a real
...e-opener.*

be with my mum and dad in the old flat in the East End of London, flying bombs and all. So after two months of living in a totally foreign environment, it was decided that I return to my blissful home in London.

Samuel Mullin was one of a family of six children, who missed out on their schooling altogether while they were away from home:

I, along with my mother, two sisters and three brothers, was – against my mother's wishes – evacuated from 17 Grove Street, Glasgow, Scotland in 1939 to Cherrybank in Perth, Scotland, leaving our father at home. He was employed as a millwright in a flour mill and was exempt from military service owing to his job. He was a volunteer ARP warden during the war and he had served with the British Army in India during 1914-18.

I was nine years of age when we were evacuated. My sister Anne was 13, my sister Jean was 10, my brother George was 12, my brother John was seven and my brother Robert was one year old.

On arrival in Perth, we were bused to an ice-hockey arena where the wooden floor was covered by straw (I believe we all spent overnight in the arena). I remember everyone was lined up and selected at random by the good folks of Cherrybank. Our complete family was then separated for the first time in our lives. Our mother and Robert were selected together, and after saying goodbye to her family, without getting any address from anyone to give to us, she was gone from the arena.

John and I were taken together by a Mr and Mrs Small to their home (Mr Small was a former Provost of Cherrybank or Perth). I do recall that they were very strict with John and me, but I also recall that they were very nice people and good to us. The first job they gave to John and me was to paint the headlights and all of the chrome on their car with black paint. (I believe it was the first car that we had ever been in.)

Our sisters, Anne and Jean, were selected together, and George was selected on his own. I remember we were all crying when we were split up, and I believe we cried for a few days afterwards.

About two weeks had gone by, and John and I were out for a walk when we saw our brother George leading cattle along with a farmer who had taken him into his home. After getting together we made some enquiries about our mother and sisters, and after a couple of days we finally all got together again as a family.

I remember our father traced us during one of his weekend visits, and he got us all together and rented a part of a house for us so we would all be a family again and together.

One day father was passing one of the newspaper buildings in Glasgow, and he looked in the view window where they used to display copies of the paper, and he noticed his six children in a news photograph all wearing clothes supplied to us in Cherrybank by the Parish Board (a board for poor families). As our father had worked steady and hard all of his life, he was fit to be tied when he saw his family wearing Parish Board clothes. I remember him telling us that he had the photograph removed from the window that day. The outfits for the boys from the Parish Board were brown herring tweed jacket and pants, black jersey with a white-trimmed collar, black socks with a white trim and black shoes; and for the girls, black gym skirt with white trim, black socks with white trim and black shoes, as I can recall.

Our father came to Cherrybank right away and made us remove the clothes, and he took them back to the Board. (In those days you could always tell what was known as a Parish family, as all the clothes were the same.)

I really can't remember how long we stayed in Cherrybank before going back to our house in Glasgow. I do know that along with my sisters and brothers we all lost about two years of education, as none of us ever attended school in Cherrybank; they did not have enough schools for all the people who were evacuated to the town.

Some evacuees were luckier than others. Not every household was anxious to have an extra body in the house – and an extra mouth to feed. Jean Schoebl (née Perkins) definitely feels she was discriminated against:

I was taken – a whole bunch of us – to Evesham [in Worcestershire] from

Birmingham. I can't remember if we went by train or bus – train, I think. What does stick out in my mind is the box of goodies they gave us – especially the huge bar of Cadbury's milk chocolate, Cadbury's chocolate biscuits and a tin of corned beef. There were other foodstuffs in the package, but the above-mentioned were the ones our hostess 'half-inched' (stole) from us!!!

The weekend immediately following our arrival, the school took us by bus to Broadway for a day's outing, and I can remember all the other kids having corned-beef sandwiches and we three poor waifs and strays having fish-paste sandwiches! Talk about 'poor relations'. The 'have-nots'!

Initially I was billeted with two other girls and we were company for one another – an adventure! We even had a pillow fight – something I'd never had the pleasure of at home! But our benefactress was never home (she had a job) when we got home from school (three houses from the school gates) and so the teachers clued in. We were moved and separated, and that was one of the most painful times of my life.

Beryl was billeted with a well-off family down by the river, and Hazel was billeted with a family that had a fruit farm. Their families were generous – with love, understanding, kindness and food!

I was billeted up the Cheltenham road, in a new area – miles, it seemed to me, out of town – with an old lady of 70 and her spinster daughter Addie of 50. *And* I was 'invited' – *let* is a better word – into their house to be their maid! Every morning before I left for school I had to 'char' – dishes, dusting, wash the floor, make their beds. And it was a *long* walk and I was so lonely walking that road every day – because all the other billetees up there were sixth-formers and me a rookie! *No one* to talk to!!!

Get this!! When they went to visit the other sister in Bengeworth, they sat down to a cooked meal at a large table and I was given a sandwich on a card table to the side. My solace was to talk to the parrot.

I felt alone, frightened, degraded, angry and constantly preached at. You can understand how I wrote home constantly imploring my father to please come and get me and I would kiss the streets of Birmingham if he did!

In contrast, for Joan Dean (now Evans), who was evacuated from London with her two sisters, the experience proved to be such a happy one that she was reluctant to go back to the city at all:

My father found out that we were going to Dunmow, in Essex, which didn't mean a thing to me. We arrived at Dunmow and were taken to the village hall, where we were put into groups, and we also had our hair

*...stling for position in
... queue for those
...cious sweet rations.*

*...oosite: College
...chers and
...olgirls in
...rtford, Kent gave
...heir holiday to
...anize a day
...sery for children
...se mothers were
...aged in war work.
...e, they hold a
...ctice parade to the
...raid shelter; they
...ed it 'going to the
...in's house'.*

inspected for fleas.

The villagers came to look us over and then they chose whom they wanted. My sisters and I were left with a couple of other families who didn't want to be split up, as my mother had told me, 'You mustn't be separated.' It seemed as if we'd stood there for hours when a Mrs Legge came and took us all. She took nine of us in. She was a very kind lady and so was her husband[!]. They owned a restaurant and cake shop, and our rooms were above the shop. We thought that was great, and were very happy there.

One evening the air-raid siren went, and we were told to come down to the cellar and put our gas-masks on. We stayed down a long time, longer than we needed to, as the all-clear had sounded but none of us heard it. But we all thought it good fun. We were all fed very well and of course had fancy cakes, which was a luxury to us. I being the eldest of the group had first pick of the cakes – that was my idea, I made that rule (I must have been horrible).

We went to the village school, and on nice sunny days we had our lessons outside, and it was lovely to see green grass and the lovely countryside. It's strange, but I never got homesick, because I loved the country and the wild flowers etc. Living in London was so dull and dreary. This was a new life. The headmaster introduced himself, but I cannot remember his name because we called him affectionately 'Daddy Trotter', as he seemed to trot and not walk. Two years ago I went back to Dunmow and asked about the headmaster; he was still alive and had gone to Canada to visit his son. The woman I spoke to said he had never forgotten the evacuees.

Alas I think we got too much for our Mrs Legge – after all, there were nine of us – so we had to move on, so my sisters and I lived with a spinster. We didn't get the freedom, and had to mind our Ps and Qs and always take our shoes off before we entered the house.

Well, we must have got her down, because once again we had to be moved. This time we did get separated; we sisters didn't like the thought of that. But as it worked out we were all very happy separated. The lady who took me was a Mrs Kirby, and her two married daughters took my sisters, so we were still within a family.

I can remember her making me a lovely cotton dress, and doing toast on the open fire. I had a huge bedroom, but there was a photograph on the wall and the eyes of the photo seemed to follow you. I mentioned this and she took the photo down. She was very kind, and her husband also; I have never forgotten her. Years after I was married, I paid her a visit and showed off my two sons and my husband; it was quite a reunion. She didn't recognize me when I knocked on her door, but she hadn't changed a bit.

I enjoyed being an evacuee. I left school at Dunmow and didn't want to come back to London, as I had made many friends. I can remember getting back home, and it was so dreary with all the windows blacked out etc., and I said, 'What a dump,' and got a clout for that remark.

Six-year-old Maureen Shotton (now Crawford) was evacuated with her sister Pamela, aged ten, from Northfleet, in Kent. They travelled by boat around the coast and arrived at Lowestoft, in Suffolk, where their first night was spent in a local cinema:

A General Steam Navigation Company information leaflet about the Royal Daffodil.

m.v. " ROYAL DAFFODIL "

1939—Evacuated 4,000 women and children from London to

We were the luckiest, having the upper foyer, which was nice and quiet. The convent school girls weren't so lucky, having to settle in a straw-covered window area in the front. All the boys were noisy brats!

Next morning, we were each given a brown paper carrier bag containing such goodies as chocolate and condensed milk. Then off we went in special buses to the various local towns and villages.

Ours was to be Diss, in Norfolk, a pretty area as I recall. We were shepherded into the local village hall to be picked out by people who would foster us. Very few wanted to take more than one evacuee. Pam and I were amongst the few kids left, when a short, hugely fat, breathless woman of about thirty exclaimed, 'Oh, I like the little one, I suppose I'll have to put up with the big one too!' So we followed Mrs Dixon back to her home.

The house was one of three attached cottages. Two rooms up and down. Upstairs was reached from a door in the parlour up narrow stairs. A tall man would have to bend his head in the rooms above. Bathroom? Well, the outside toilet was shared by the other two houses and we were the furthest away! Which 'lady' of the houses cleaned it out I don't know, but I'm sure it wasn't ours. My mother reckoned she never did *any* cleaning! But boy, she loved our chocolate. We never did get to know how it tasted!

Mr Dixon, her husband, was a dear. A skinny man, he was off by 6 a.m. each morning to work at a local pig farm. That's when Mrs Dixon cooked our breakfast of egg and bacon too. She was annoyed that we didn't like it cold at 7.30 a.m. when we had our breakfast.

Next door there was another evacuee, who came from London. Ruth was about a year older than me. She was a nice quiet little girl living with a young couple who had a spoilt brat of a three-year-old daughter. Ruth was obviously very affected by the evacuation, as she constantly wet her panties. She never said anything to us, but my sister suspected, and later discovered that the foster mother sent her to school without any knickers as a punishment.

When my mother came to visit us, I cried as I sat in school, convinced she'd get lost. A kind teacher comforted me, and sure enough, there was my mummy waiting for me when school was over. She laughingly confessed that she had indeed lost herself, going past the churchyard three times to hear the same old gent say, 'Mornin' Ma'am,' at each passing.

Just a few weeks later I arrived back from school to find my mother sitting in the front parlour with a strange man. I chattered away to my mummy, showing her all the craftwork I'd done that day. 'Don't you know this gentleman?' my mother asked. I'd been very aloof to this smiling man with my mummy, whilst my daddy was away. 'It's your

Daddy!' I hadn't seen him for about a year. No, I didn't recognize the man who had rushed back to England (by boat in those days). I suppose it was all the shock of being evacuated that caused me not to recognize him. My sister's reaction on the other hand was very different. As we walked towards her coming home from school, she screamed 'Daddy!' and rushed, jumping into his arms – sure made up for my cool reception!

This was just six weeks after we'd left home. Next day we were taken back to Northfleet. On the long bus trip home I remember my mother being aghast at discovering the huge safety-pin holding up my knickers. I thought it was great!

Amazingly, it took me weeks to really accept that this was indeed my beloved daddy back home. I even thought HE was getting to the postal delivery and 'pinching' my daddy's letters before my mummy could see them! What a confused little girl I must have been.

My sister was later evacuated again, this time to Newton Abbot, in Devon. She stayed there (with another girl) for several months, at the home of a widow of an army general. They were cared for by the house-keeper, often having afternoon tea with the lady of the house. Pam had a wonderful time there, returning home quite the little lady. My parents decided to have her back home, as they felt if we were going to die, we might as well be close together.

I was never evacuated again, spending many hours of tuition in school shelters. Although I was obviously profoundly affected by the evacuation, those six weeks I'm sure have played a large part in making me the strong, compassionate person I am today.

May Renardson (now Tate), who went to stay not far from York, ended up being one of quite a houseful:

It's hard to remember too many details, but I remember waiting to get on the bus with my name-tag attached to my coat and my gas-mask hanging in its box around my neck. My mother was seeing me off; it sure must have been hard for her to send her youngest away. I was thirteen, and had been ill with rheumatic fever when I was ten and missed a whole year of schooling, so wasn't very strong. I was too embarrassed to kiss her good-bye.

The Preston family from Moreby Hall took seven of us, and a Mrs Dickinson with her two children looked after us all. We were in the ser-vants' quarters, so had a lovely place, and the grounds went down to the River Ouse. We had to walk 1½ miles to the school in Stillingfleet and we had our hot meal at a farmhouse at noon. I can still remember the dum-plings we had for dessert served with syrup.

We didn't see much of the Preston family. Mrs Preston's husband was

*ay Renardson
(standing) and other
children taken in by
the Preston family
having lunch at a
farmhouse in
Killingfleet, Yorkshire.*

a colonel in the Army. They had two daughters, Miss Josephine and Miss Felicity. Two sisters joined us, so that made eleven of us. We all got head lice. So poor Mrs Dickinson had to small-tooth comb the eleven of us daily until we got rid of them.

Doreen Wilson (née Pooley) writes that she is surprised at how much she remembers:

I was not yet four and my brother only a couple of years older, so when we were lined up in the local schoolyard to be readied for our journey into the unknown we were accompanied by our mother. I'm quite amazed at how vivid are my recollections of that day and the ones to follow.

We eventually, after what seemed like a very long journey, found

*Doreen Pooley and
other evacuees
playing in the
schoolyard in
Taunton, Somerset,
1940.*

ourselves billed in the servants' quarters of a well-known brewer in Merstham, Surrey – which seems surprisingly close to London when you drive there today. My mother felt very uncomfortable there, not really welcome either by the servants or by the family, and we only stayed a few weeks. A distant relative in Somerset, suddenly discovering that she had to take in evacuees, decided that we would be better than total strangers, and invited us to Taunton.

There we discovered a horde of kids from an East London school, who had been evacuated *en bloc*, and who were viewed with a somewhat jaundiced eye by the worthy matrons of that lovely but rather staid county town. My brother immediately teamed up with a small group of active East Enders, who taught him all kinds of new tricks, and my mother rapidly turned grey. Being one of the very few London mothers there, she seemed to feel responsible for the behaviour of the whole bunch!

Other recollections crowd into my mind: lining up in the schoolyard in Taunton for our daily dollop of cod-liver oil and malt; parties at the local restaurant with jelly and blancmange (rare treats); competing with my brother to learn the silhouettes of all Allied and enemy aircraft from the chart on the wall; listening to the daily radio news filled with the casualty figures, and vaguely wondering what they would talk about if there hadn't been a war on; hiring a man to come and take up the floorboards to recover a precious half-crown which had slipped down between the cracks, and sharing the retrieved treasure with him; and of course THE BOMB, which was jettisoned by a retreating German bomber and killed a couple of cows in a nearby field!

For Margaret Crawford (now Trayling), who was evacuated at the age of eight, the experience was to have long-lasting effects:

My only lifeline was my cousin – but he was a boy, and people did not want one of each sex if they took you in. However, as we were the last two left in the classroom (and it had been a long and strange day), this lady Mrs Ridgeway decided she would take us. She had a box-room and a single bed. We did not mind; we had a roof, a bed and people who seemed to like us, so we settled – for a few months.

Now Mrs Ridgeway's daughter was going to have a baby, quite a normal thing to happen, but she wanted to move back home while her husband was in the Navy. She wanted our room, our bed, all because of this baby.

I resented this soon-to-come new arrival. Where was it? Where was it coming from? I couldn't see it, and yet it was causing disruption and taking from us our only bit of security.

Dear Dad

    I hope you well and happy. I had a letter from Grany Grawford and Farfy and Aunty Queenie with a 2/- post alorder in it. I go to chuch every sunday and they give me a little stamp and a book to put it in. Down our road there is a sweel shop and the lady nows me she gave me a Bag of Broken up sweet. When Gran Wrote she said if she come down to see me she might unsettle me. wrich made me laugh. and Aunty said She can come. Gran Asked if I was

ill or Fretin I am nott ill or Fretin. do you like being a solder. Mum says She misses you very much I still go to The Picturse evre week Lafs of Love and Kissi's. Love from MRAGARET XX X X X X X X X X X

Dad X
Dad X

garet Crawford writes to her father.

105

Margaret Crawford (in the front row, wearing a beret) and schoolfriends.

My cousin was moved to another foster home. This invisible baby had got us out and taken my lifeline away. More resentment built up towards babies.

I was moved to the other end of the same road, where this lady had a baby of six months old, and there I became the drudge, never allowed to play out, forever doing a chore for this baby, even ironing its nappies. Oh I did not like babies. Never did I hurt or injure this child, but to me they made nasty things happen, and made you sad. I made my mind up there and then I would not have any, wherever they came from.

But after years of thinking I had no maternal instincts, and eight years of marriage, I found the feelings were there. But my son never knew the traumas of insecurity.

Rita Wright (née Gabrelovitch) remembers one very beneficial aspect of her evacuation:

A school photograph of Rita Gabrelovitch, aged 9.

For my part, the one really good thing about being evacuated to the countryside was the fact that my health improved so much. Although my parents had fed me well, because of our crowded living conditions at home I suffered from bronchial pneumonia every winter and had done so since I was a baby; but from the time I was evacuated I never suffered again from this illness. I would also think that the abundance and availability of locally grown fresh fruit and vegetables kept me very healthy.

During the first summer of the war, and before the Blitz started, I returned home to the East End of London for a little holiday, with rosy cheeks and a tan, and quite a few people commented, 'I bet she's an evacuee!'

I was so proud!

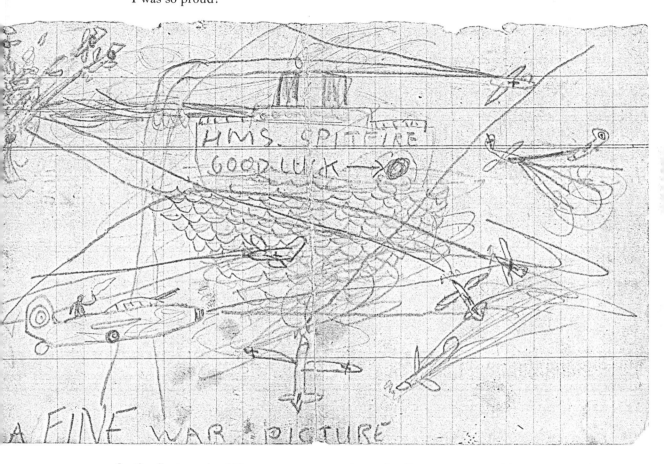

'A fine war picture' drawn by Rita Gabrelovitch on the back of her school geography notes.

As the first week of the war came to a close, the Government could look back with some satisfaction on what had been an extremely successful evacuation of mothers and children to areas that were considered to be safe.

More than a million children, clutching gas-masks and emergency rations, had marched on to railway platforms and into bus stations and ferry ports, bound for unknown destinations, and no casualties had been reported.

From Downing Street, the evacuation scheme appeared to be a success.

4
WHAT
WAR?

For those who were expecting an all-out war, the opening months of the conflict were a bore. The troops in France found themselves with little to do other than stare in the direction of where the enemy were staring back.

Many mothers who had left their homes in the city began to return with their children. What was the point of living in strange surroundings, without the familiar pub and fish-and-chip shop, in order to be safe from bombs, if no bombs were falling?

Veronica Knight (now Nottingham), who was evacuated with her brother from Wythenshawe, Manchester, to Glossop, on the edge of the Pennines, was away for just three months:

My little family consisted of the parents, Bert and Clara, and a delightful wee son named John. How welcome they made me; it was just as if I had been part of their family all my life. My younger brother was billeted three houses away with a dear young couple. I was just twelve years old

The pressure exerted on mothers to send their children away – and keep them away – was reinforced by government posters, which often amounted to little more than emotional blackmail.

and my brother was five, and I can honestly say they were three of the happiest months of my life.

The small village school was stretched to accommodate us – as I recall, we attended on a part-time basis. Amongst others, the music teacher there (even though I have forgotten his name) remains in my memory and I see him in my mind's eye. I'm sure he must have been called out of retirement. He fostered and encouraged a love of music in me which still remains.

What a trial we city children must have been to all the teachers at the small school, including the few who had accompanied me, who un-stintingly gave of their time, and knowledge, all with patience and under-standing. The little (then) town was also a delightful place, especially for city children, the countryside and slower pace being a pleasure to me.

Just before Christmas 1939, owing to changing circumstances, the couple who had my brother could no longer accommodate him, and so with many, many tears and heartache, on my part especially, we returned to Manchester. By this time Wythenshawe had been declared a safe area, and no children were to be officially evacuated – the few children who had initially been sent to Shropshire returned because of the 'safe' ruling.

Ironically, as the war progressed, our area was bombed (mistakenly I believe) and a land mine was deposited quite near to Northenden golf course. This caused great excitement amongst all the young ones and, despite dire warnings from officials and parents, hordes of us cycled to 'the village' to view the huge crater and wonder at all the goings-on!!

Unfortunately, in April 1940, the 'phoney war' came to an end. German troops crossed the borders of Norway and Denmark, forcing the Allied troops to retreat in the face of Hitler's rapidly advancing army.

With the resignation of Neville Chamberlain in May, Winston Churchill became Prime Minister. 'I have nothing to offer but blood, toil, tears and sweat,' he told a packed House of Commons in a speech that was to become famous throughout the world.

Rotterdam was destroyed by the German air force, with the loss of more than a thousand lives. The Allies continued to fall back in France, forcing Churchill's Government to rethink an evacuation scheme that had sent thousands of children to 'safe' havens on Britain's south coast. Many of these children were in danger of finding themselves in the front line, closer to the enemy than anyone else in the country.

All London children who in 1939 had been evacuated to areas within a ten-mile zone inland along the coast from Norfolk to Sussex were re-evacuated to South Wales and the Midlands. Those who had gone back to their homes in areas in the designated danger zone began to feel

British troops being evacuated from the beach at Dunkirk, June 1940.

that they might have made a mistake. The Battle of Britain was imminent and Churchill's prophecy in the House of Commons in June that this would be remembered as Britain's 'finest hour' did little to ease their fears. The first attack on British soil had occurred on 10 May at the hand of a solitary German plane.

The British Army was forced to retreat to Dunkirk, on the northern coast of France, from where its soldiers made their way back across the Channel aboard small boats and fishing vessels and by any other means they could find.

A headline in the *Daily Mirror* said it all: 'BLOODY MARVELLOUS'.

And it was. More than 300,000 troops had been lifted from the beaches and brought safely back to England.

British Expeditionary Force troopships leaving a French port for England to assist in the defence of the homeland.

For Sidney Chapman, who had been sent to live in Weymouth, in Dorset, the evacuation of Dunkirk certainly proved to be an eye-opener:

Unexpectedly, we saw the effects of war before our parents in London did. The experience of being away from home like this gave many of us opportunities to assume responsibilities that would not otherwise have come our way.

In May, when Hitler's armies were advancing across France, Weymouth became a reception area for the French troops and civilians who had escaped across the Channel in a variety of small boats. A number of us were recruited to make use of our limited grammar-school French and help receive these people and compile lists of their names and origins.

In early July, while some of us were cycling to school, we had a ringside view of a German dive-bomb attack on nearby Portland naval base. Frequently school activity was disrupted by air-raid sirens signalling the approach of enemy aircraft. But most of the time they were heading for

French soldiers and marines who had fought the heroic rearguard action at Dunkirk are welcomed with refreshments on their arrival in England.

other centres like Bristol.

Final examinations were written in July and, not surprisingly, on more than one occasion the writing was interrupted by air-raid sirens. Students were paraded off to air-raid shelters, being admonished not to discuss the exams, and then resumed writing when the all-clear went.

Patricia MacDonald (née Jones), who was evacuated from Old Trafford, Manchester, has colourful memories of her uncle who, after being wounded at Dunkirk, came to look after Patricia and her brother:

When the war broke out in September 1939, my mother rented a cottage in Knutsford, Cheshire, so that my brother Terry and I would not have to put up with just 'anybody' in the evacuation of Manchester. It was a lovely cottage – it was about 400 years old and stood on the outskirts of the village of Knutsford, a truly beautiful place. Across the road from our cottage was the home of some 'gentleman' who had gone off to the war and left his 'estate' for evacuees. It was a lovely big stately home, the sort of place kids like me and my brother had only seen on postcards. We used to look at it every day on our way to the little schoolhouse, which was in Knutsford. It was a Catholic school and therefore it was very small – two rooms for all of us, and two teachers. It must have been ideal for the few Catholic kids of Knutsford at that time, but when the evacuees started to arrive from Manchester, Liverpool and London it was really crowded. Anyway, my brother Terry and I didn't mind it, as the teacher treated all evacuees the same way – with much distaste, as did most of the residents of this lovely English village. We were blamed for everything – bad manners, vandalism, swearing – you name it, we were blamed for it all.

Anyway, in 1940 my uncle, who had been wounded at Dunkirk, came to look after my brother and me so that my mother could return to Manchester and be with my father, whose work was so important to the war effort that he was not taken into the Army. He worked for Vickers, and he told me later he worked on Asdic, which we now call radar.

About the same time as my Uncle Mick came to take care of my brother and me, the lovely 'estate' across the road from us was taken over by a bunch of evacuees from Trafford Park, Manchester. There were about twelve kids and they had a sort of 'house mother', a woman who had a couple of babies; she was supposed to supervise the kids while getting the run of the place at the same time. My brother Terry and I were delighted at the prospect of having some kids our age (seven to thirteen) living across the road from us – especially in the house we had long admired!

Well, my brother and I soon became such good friends of the Trafford

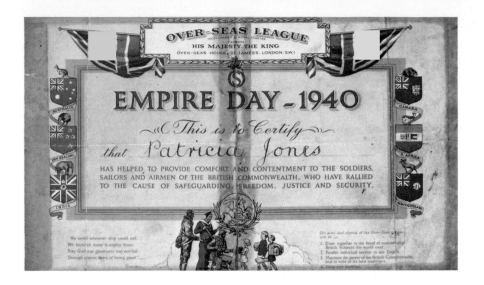

OVER-SEAS LEAGUE

INCORPORATED BY ROYAL CHARTER

PATRON

HIS MAJESTY THE KING

OVER-SEAS HOUSE, ST. JAMES'S, LONDON. S.W.1

EMPIRE DAY ~ 1940

This is to Certify

that **Patricia Jones**

HAS HELPED TO PROVIDE COMFORT AND CONTENTMENT TO THE SOLDIERS, SAILORS AND AIRMEN OF THE BRITISH COMMONWEALTH, WHO HAVE RALLIED TO THE CAUSE OF SAFEGUARDING FREEDOM, JUSTICE AND SECURITY.

Park evacuees that we were invited over all the time – we even slept in that lovely old mansion the odd time. The house was even more beautiful inside than it was from the outside, with wide staircases going upstairs to magnificent bedrooms – and everything painted white. I'd never seen the likes of it before, only in Shirley Temple pictures at the Trafford, where I used to go before the war every Saturday afternoon. The hall was wide and spacious, and there were so many rooms downstairs that you couldn't believe your eyes. God, I didn't know there was such bloody luxury in the world. I remember thinking to myself how I must be in some sort of dream and I would wake up any minute and be back in my simple little working-man's house on the housing estate in Old Trafford. The only reason my mother rented the cottage at Knutsford was because she was scared of the air raids herself and wanted to get out of the way. She couldn't really afford it – we were always in dutch for the rent, and it was only her good looks and glib tongue that kept the old landlord from throwing us out!

My brother Terry and I seemed to spend more time over the road in the mansion than we did in our cottage, where my Uncle Mick was always digging the garden to make an air-raid shelter for our safety. The odd time he would go out at night and pinch some vegetables from the farm near us and make Irish stew for our dinner the next day.

Although Uncle Mick had spent most of his life in the British Army, he was an Irishman by birth. He was a loving and kind gentleman; my brother Terry and I loved him most of our lives. He used to sit beside the fire and tell us stories about his adventures in the Army. I would close my eyes and almost relive the stories with him. He had been all over the world – especially India, where he had been for years before the outbreak of the war. He hated the war we were in, he loathed the way the Germans bombed innocent women and children. He couldn't understand the way children had to leave their homes to seek safety in the country. He used to

A certificate awarded to Patricia Jones while she was at school in Knutsford. Every afternoon, as the teacher read the girls their lessons, they sat and knitted. In each finished balaclava, Patricia would slip a little note, which usually read 'I love you, from Pat Jones'.

tell us stories about World War I, when men fought practically 'face to face' – but with a certain amount of honour. He said World War I (he was then in his twenties and fought at the front with the Lancashire Fusiliers) was a dreadful waste of life. How true his words ring in my ears today.

But in the times I am trying to write about he had come to the end of his days as a soldier, and would not live to see the end of World War II... I didn't know it then... nor did he, as he tried so hard to 'recover' from his wounds from Dunkirk. He was looking forward to 'recovering' so that he would be able to take out his hate on the rotten Germans who had caused all this. The way he dug that shelter for my brother and me – I'll never forget him. His love of a country he hadn't even been born in. His love and compassion for children – especially for children: my brother and I could bring the whole school home if we wanted and he would make up a nice meal and make them feel loved and cared for. My brother and I were much envied by lots of kids for having such a great man to care for us all.

There was somebody else who had an 'eye' on him too, and it wasn't a kid – it was the lady across the road who lived in the mansion. One day she asked me if I could get my uncle over to help her open a door that led from the massive kitchen to the basement. My uncle was the obliging sort anyway, so I only had to ask him once and he was more than willing to oblige. In the meantime, my brother and I were busy helping the other kids dig a trench that ran the length of the tennis court. Boy, that red gravel was hard to dig up – but we did it. You should have seen the tennis court when we had finished!

Inside the mansion my uncle had opened the heavy oak door that led to the cellar – the wine cellar to be more precise. While my uncle and his lady tasted the grapes of the vine and got so bloody drunk, the ack-ack batteries had moved into a field beside our own cottage. They made a hell of a noise trying to 'down' German bombers who were on their way to bomb Manchester or Liverpool. They wanted to get the bombers before they could reach the cities.

My uncle was so drunk he didn't know what bleeding war he was in! This little spree of his and his lady-friend's lasted for at least three days. In the meantime, after we kids had finished digging up the tennis court, we then decided to play indoors. We opened glass cases where safari outfits had been placed on display, as well as old British Army uniforms. We all got done up and ran around the mansion pretending it was the Somme or Cambrai; we had gas attacks and it was man-to-man fighting all the way through the library, the drawing room, the dining room – there was silver everywhere!

We all wore medals (taken from another display cabinet); we were in a patriotic fever as we fought from room to room. It was England we were fighting for. It was 'over the top' all the way – right out into the gardens, where another regiment of our soliders had dug deep into the once lovely flower beds (the trenches ran all around the mansion). What a glorious battle it was. England won the war.

My brother and I had to practically carry Uncle Mick back to the cottage. As it turned out there was an air raid that night, and as my brother and I were put into the shelter my uncle had made for us, he was very angry (and still half 'cut') and he stood in the garden and started cursing up to the skies where the German bombers were sort of 'low flying'. It was a lovely moonlit night, and between my uncle calling the Germans all the lousy bastards that ever walked the earth and the ack-ack firing from close by, it was indeed a night to remember.

When Uncle Mick had sobered up and saw the state of the mansion across the road, he wanted to get drunk again – but he didn't. But he did take another drink one night, and as he held up the glass, he looked over at my brother and me as we sat before the fire in our cottage in Knutsford, and for once in a sober state I heard him swear... 'Here's to that poor bastard who left his home to the evacuees of Manchester. He left his home to fight for England... his home... by Christ, I hope he doesn't regret it when he comes back!'

On 10 June 1940 Mussolini declared war on the Allies. On 14 June the Germans entered Paris, and on 22 June an armistice between France and Germany was signed.

Britain was left to fight alone.

One of the most visible signs that the population was now becoming more conscious than ever of the danger was an increase in the number of people who carried their gas-masks with them.

To pre-empt any plans the Germans might have had for capturing the BBC and 'planting' their own announcers, all newsreaders began their broadcasts by identifying themselves: 'Here is the news and this is Frank Phillips reading it.'

The ringing of church bells was reserved for emergencies, and from the end of July, the Local Defence Volunteers were re-formed as the Home Guard.

Dora Hewitt (now Hefler)'s father joined the Home Guard and stayed in London, while the rest of the family were evacuated:

I was the eldest of four kids in our family. I remember we were taken with our dear mother to some London school, given a gas-mask each and a carrier bag with some chocolate and biscuits, and lined up and marched to some railway station (can't remember the names). We all arrived in

children whose
wartime reality was
evacuation to the
peace and safety of
the countryside, other
aspects of the war
were often no more
than a game.

Leicester, a place called Oadby, where we were met by some council members and they decided where we should all live. I remember my sister and I were in one house (very posh), and my little brother – he was about five I think – was in another house, as his so-called foster parents only wanted boys – no girls – to be billeted with them, and my mother and baby sister in arms went to another very posh place, where they thought my mother would be their maid (bloody cheek).

Well, after living in those different homes, my sister, who had never sat on a horse in her life, met with a tragic horse accident: she fell off a horse and was dragged for miles along a country road. She was admitted to hospital with so much wrong with her leg that it troubles her even to this day; she's always been in and out of hospital over the years as a result of our evacuation. Doctors wanted to amputate her leg, and one day, back in the London Hospital in Whitechapel, London, my mother sat all day just waiting for this wonderful doctor (who has since been knighted Sir Reginald Watson Jones), and he did this first operation on my sister's leg, and we were told it's all in the *Guinness Book of Records* or the *British Journal*.

Well, between Leicester and my mother running back to London to be with our father, who was an air-raid warden at the time, and then losing our house to the bombs etc. etc., my mother and all four kids were then taken to Wales, a place called Abertillery. Those Welsh people were very kind towards us. Once more we were all split up in different homes. I remember vividly every Sunday my mother would buy a leg of lamb or roast beef, just so as she could have us all four kids together sitting down to eat, which meant having her landlady and family too.

Finally when it was reasonably safe for us to come back to London, those doodlebugs dropped on us, and my father rented a place in Laindon, Essex, where we all lived until the war was over.

Altogether we were bombed out in London twice, then again in Dagenham, Essex, several more times. I even remember my mother giving us a pram with all our blankets and some food, hurrying over to the park air-raid shelters and finding a place for all five of us to sleep. She would come over later, as she always had some blooming chores to do.

After a few months of being with the Home Guard, my father refused to go on the roof-tops to watch for the Germans, as he wasn't one of the lucky officers who were given boots and a waterproof mackintosh, so he quit. We all had a good laugh over this and thought for sure he would be put in prison.

P.S. Just remembered, at the time of our first evacuation we were living in Stoke Newington, London, N16. Can't help having a little tiddle (cry) as I'm writing this.

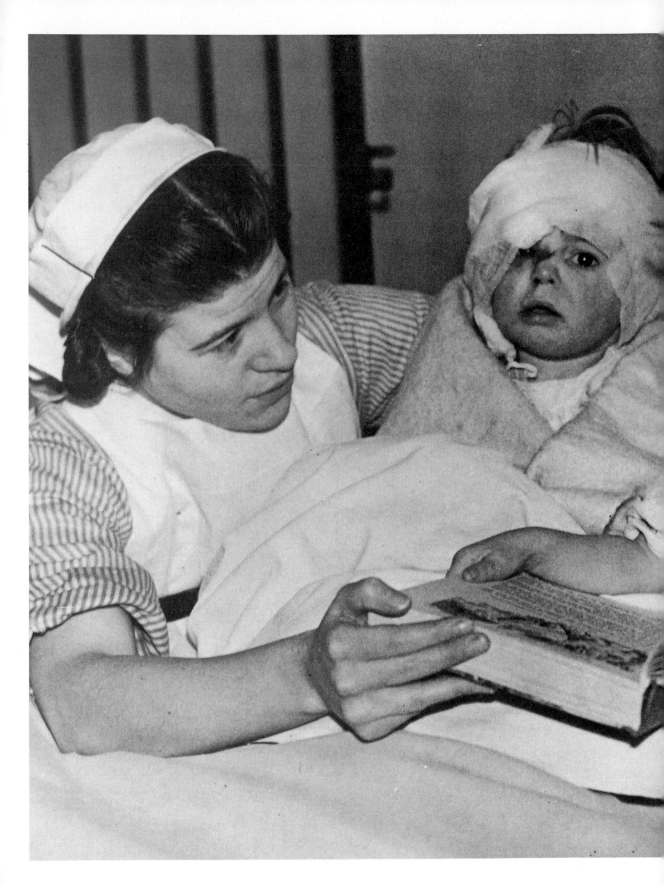

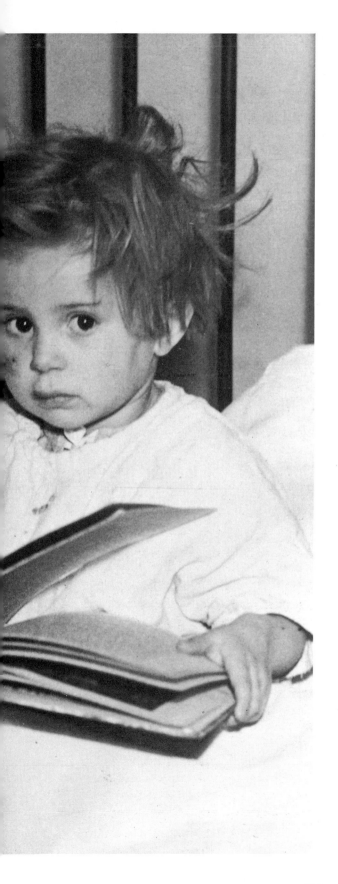

5
THE
BATTLE
OF
BRITAIN

The official date for the beginning of the Battle of Britain is fixed at 10 July 1940, although German aircraft had been busy bombing convoys on their way through the straits of Dover long before this.

On 10 July a BBC reporter was reading from a prepared script when a dogfight took place overhead. His energetic report had all the colour and tone of a sports commentary, and with his enthusiastic 'Oh boy, I've never seen anything so good as this . . .', the whole country was suddenly aware that it had a front-row seat for the spectacle of a major battle.

In the months that followed, the number of enemy aircraft increased, and air raids became more frequent and more widely spread. Ben Banham was a member of the inspection staff of the Birmingham fire brigade. When the bombing became so bad that the city's water supply was threatened, many children, including his two young daughters, were evacuated:

I was charged with the duty of visiting all theatres, music halls, cinemas and any premises carrying a music, singing or dancing licence, including pubs (they were the best).

I was on a cinema circuit and chatting with the manager in his office, when a girl usher walked in and reported that a man was sitting in the ninepenny seats on a sixpenny ticket. The manager, about five foot six, went out to investigate and came back laughing his head off. When asked how he'd got on, he said he had tapped the fellow on the shoulder and told him to move. 'The guy started to stand up, and Jesus, I thought he would never stop getting up. He was about six foot eight, so I patted his back and told him, "That's all right old man, you're all right where you are."'

Our three children and Mum spent scores of nights in the Anderson shelter in the garden, which I had dug in and sandbagged. I, of course, was out dealing with the results of Gerry's handiwork.

On November 22nd, 1940, we suffered the longest raid of the war – 13 hours. Early in the raid a bomb dropped between twin 36-inch water mains on the Bristol Road near Northfield. These mains carried the majority of Birmingham's water from the Elan Valley in Wales. Most of the city was without mains water for many days, some areas I think two weeks.

This was the signal for the city to evacuate the schoolchildren. Our daughters Muriel, seven, and Irene, five, went with their teachers to Treherbert in the Rhondda Valley. They went with an army blanket rolled and slung over their shoulders and a suitcase of clothing. Our son Rag was too young to go.

Inconsolable: children of the Raphael Mackinnon School in Deptford, London on their return from the East Grinstead district of Sussex.

In London's East End, an ARP warden helps homeless mothers and babies to move to a safer place.

Some parents couldn't stand the parting and soon started to fetch the kids home. We left ours until the following May and then, as things had quietened down, I borrowed a friend's Morris Minor and a few petrol coupons and drove down to Treherbert and met the very nice miner and his family with whom we had corresponded. I remember buying two gallons of paraffin to put in the car as I wondered whether the gas coupons would get us back to Brum.

Our biggest surprise was that our daughters were speaking with a pure Welsh accent (which rather quickly wore off).

Doris Groves (now Bauer) was evacuated twice:

The first time, my whole school was evacuated. We were sent from Dagenham, Essex, to Northampton. We left the school grounds very early one morning in March 1939, and all boarded buses with knapsacks on our backs. All were given a bar of dark chocolate and a tin of corned beef. I have often wondered about that tin of corned beef – were we supposed to eat it? Whenever I open one I think about that. That's all we

had, however, that day. I remember eating the chocolate.

My sister and I were together; I was nine years, she was nearly six. I can still see my mum waving us goodbye with my baby sister in her arms. I've often tried to imagine how she must have felt that day as two of her children were leaving her side, and she not knowing when she was going to see us again – and she also not knowing at that time where my soldier dad was. She hid her tears from us, hugging us to be brave.

We arrived in Northampton that evening; it seemed to take such a long time. We were taken to a big hall and told to stand and wait. As a child I felt the indignity of that wait and what was to come. I will never forget the way I felt as people stood over us picking and choosing from us children, pointing at us. I was told pointing was rude as a child growing up.

It seemed to take so long. Most only wanted one evacuee. I was adamant, with a protective arm about my little sister, who was crying and asking for her mummy; I refused to be parted from her. Evelyn and I were so tired of standing so long. I didn't cry; I was, I remember, experiencing a much stronger feeling – not wanting to be separated from her. I held on to her very tightly, until finally we were the only two children standing there. There were about five or six adults; I remember distinctly they were discussing us and where we should go. Evelyn was finally pulled from my arms – *then* I cried so hard, struggling and sobbing.

It was dark when the lady who finally took me and I arrived at her home. I didn't know where Evelyn had gone. I was sobbing so hard I could hardly breathe, and was perspiring; the lady was wiping my forehead – she had long red fingernails, I remember. I had a sudden idea I would write to Mum; all the time I was pleading for her to take me to Evelyn and to go home. I remember she didn't speak at all and answer my questions. I asked her for a pen, paper and a stamp, and wrote a short note to my mum to please bring us home. I remember running out in the dark to find a letter box, doing so and running back. When I got there, the lady wasn't home. When she finally came, she told me she would take me to live with my sister who was just six houses away. I felt that much better for knowing she was near and I could go to her and be with her.

I have thought so often of how my mum must have felt receiving that note from me, and if she really did. At an appropriate time I will ask her. The times we have discussed those war years and the partings Mum isn't very talkative. I realize that now, as a mother, those times were too hurtful to talk about. My dad also was a soft-hearted, warm, loving person – an exceptional dad. He must have been very hurt by it all, being dragged from us, at times not knowing where we were.

In the home my sister and I stayed in, I was treated OK in the ensuing months, but I knew Evelyn was not. She cried a lot for her mummy; they

o German Dornier mbers flying above s started by bombs pped in the ghbourhood of yal Victoria Dock d Silvertown, East ndon during the ttle of Britain. The otograph, taken m the attacking craft and now in possession of the F, shows how ndon appeared to Luftwaffe crews.

would send me out of the room and spank her, but I knew and could hear it. I would run back and cry my protest, but it still went on. A few months later we were preparing for Christmas, and my mum and dad were coming to see us. When they came, Dad was dressed in his army 'blues'; he obviously had leave to come and see us. My mum and dad took one look at us and knew they would be taking us home with them. We were so happy. When Dad had to go back to the army barracks in Larkhill, Salisbury, Wiltshire, we were so sad. I remember seeing tears in my mum's eyes; she would try to hide them from us.

The raids and bombings were so bad that we lived most of the time in our air-raid shelter in our garden. We couldn't possibly continue that way. My mum would bring us in from play about 6 p.m., and we were all in bed soon after – not just in the same bedroom but in the same bed! Mum wouldn't let us out of her sight.

I remember one day she had to go to buy some food, and she took Barbara, our baby, in a pushchair. She told me that when the siren went I was to run to the shelter with Evelyn and wait for her to return. As usual, the siren went, and I did as she said. Suddenly, there was Mum climbing in the shelter, so out of breath, with Barbara, throwing the pushchair to the ground; her shins were bleeding where she had banged them on the pushchair while running. I remember that so vividly. She hugged us three to her until the all-clear siren blew.

All families in that area for safety reasons had to evacuate, so Mum and all of us did so together this time. Our neighbour was a young bride of a soldier; away she came along with us and tried to stay with us. I remember we travelled on a train, and arrived somewhere in Norfolk. I remember we were assembled in a big hall, and that night we all slept on the floor; that hall was packed. I don't think any of the mothers slept that night; I didn't either. There was so much sadness, so many tears. Then mothers were singing; they sang a lot. One song I remember was sung over and over: 'Pack up your troubles in your old kit bag and smile, smile, smile.'

The next day once again I witnessed in my young life being chosen for a home, and once again was unlucky to be without my loved ones. I was taken against my mum's wishes, and pleading, alone to a home in the country, not knowing where my mum and sisters went; that was again a tearful time for my mum and me. We stayed there three weeks; then one day my mum turned up at the home where I was, with my sisters and another lady with her three children. She took me and said we were going home once again. We were all so happy.

We came home to a rather quiet town, a rather bombed town, with houses and business missing. We said goodbye to Mum's friend that she

Children watch a dogfight from a trench in the hopfields of Kent during the Battle of Britain.

had made in that time away, and we walked home to our house, which fortunately was still standing. Suddenly, happily, Dad came home on leave. He came home regularly after that. He always brought us his sweet ration – and we saved him ours! I thought he was so brave when at times he would stand outside the air-raid shelter and watch the enemy planes flying over and bombing in the distance. He would jump in when it was 'close'.

John Stonehewer was born and grew up in Barry, a seaport about twelve miles from Cardiff, South Wales:

We had our share of army camps, British and US. The beaches were spiked to discourage landing-craft, and cordoned off to the general public. If I remember correctly, on one headland at the end of the main beach there was a genuine anti-aircraft battery. The other headland had a much larger emplacement, completely false, to fool the enemy. I used to think it was a good idea, and unique to Barry, but over the years I've read about many similar fabrications.

My folks thought Barry would be hit hard, as we were near the large docks at Cardiff, and not really too far from the English Channel, well within range of German bombers. My folks figured Manchester was so much further from Germany that they sent my brother (three years my junior) and me to stay with relatives in Manchester. Not the same family either. We were at different ends of the city. I missed my parents terribly, and seldom saw my brother either.

So here we were, far from home, presumably safer. Fiddlesticks (or some such expression). I don't think there was a night when I wasn't taken from bed, either to someone's cellar or to the air-raid shelter in the middle of the street. When the all-clear went, out we'd come, stand and watch the city on fire, and go home to bed. Many times, in the morning, one of the houses on the street would be gone. My brother fared the same, where he stayed.

I've always thought it was one and a half years later (maybe it was less) that I finally wrote home and asked them to come and get us. They did. Barry had hardly been damaged. A couple of mines had been dropped, and some bombs.

The siren sounded many nights when we were home, and we'd sit in the back-garden Anderson shelter, with government-issue plugs in our ears and rubber between our teeth. I remember being scared at times, at the anti-aircraft fire and the occasional bomb, but mostly the noise was from dogfights between the fighter planes.

We had our shrapnel collections, and at school, if the siren sounded, we'd go down below, and the teacher would read *Just William* books. If we were over half-way to school when the alarm went off, we were supposed to run straight to school. Less than half-way, we were supposed to go back home. But even if we were outside the school door, we'd go the mile and a half back home anyway.

I remember standing and watching the daytime dogfights over the Bristol Channel, and cheering when a German plane went down.

Jacqueline Pickering (now Baird) was evacuated with her mother and two sisters from Portsmouth, in Hampshire:

In 1941 Portsmouth was being heavily bombed, almost nightly I believe, owing to its being a large naval base, and it was therefore necessary to start evacuation. We had already said goodbye to my father for five years, and so, along with my mother, six-year-old sister and two-month-old sister, I set off for a little village called Meonstoke, set in the Meon Valley, Hampshire. I would add that my youngest sister, who was a breech birth, had been delivered under the stairs during an air raid.

We arrived in Meonstoke and were sent to the Absolem family. Wonderful Mrs Absolem already had three children of her own, but she welcomed the four of us with open arms. It was a very modest house, but it had a front garden – we just had a forecourt in Portsmouth, which was only useful when boredom set in and we played gingerbread. Going from a terraced house in Portsmouth, in a street with no trees, to a place like Meonstoke to me was like going to heaven. Green fields, trees, fish in streams – and cows! We actually milked a cow.

My older sister and I were sent off to school, I imagine to give my poor mother a break. It was just a one-room school, and everybody was very friendly. I learned to knit! We went on field trips, which I thought were the best thing that could happen to anybody – until I stepped in a cow pat. However, my mother made me feel better when she said I would have to step in something worse than that before I died.

We lived on Meonstoke for about a year and then, for reasons still not quite clear to me, were obliged to move back to Portsmouth. My evacuation story really ends here, but I will carry on.

The city was still being heavily bombed, and ironically the last bomb to fall fell on my aunt's house in the next road. We were all in the underground garden shelter at the time, although my mother and youngest sister were late going down and so suffered minor injuries. I couldn't believe what had happened – houses flattened, rubble everywhere and a baby dead across the road. However, that didn't stop 'our gang' rushing around collecting shrapnel.

Jacqueline Pickering's grandparents visit Meonstoke. In the back row are Jackie's baby sister Ann, her mother and her grandparents, and in front, Jackie and her sister Sheila.

6
THE
BLITZ
BEGINS

The first daylight raid on London took place in August 1940. Britain's Bomber Command retaliated by dropping bombs on Berlin.

The war on the capital cities had begun. Many people who had remained at home now felt it was time – or were compelled by the bombing – to move away. Stella Doy (now Kendall) was evacuated to Great Horwood, in Buckinghamshire, along with her mother and sister:

After being bombed out of two homes in South London, my parents heard of one old lady in Buckinghamshire who was prepared to share her cottage with my mother, my sister and me while my father worked in an ammunitions factory in London.

Maybe being the only evacuees in the village was the reason for being so unkindly treated by the other children. Having read accounts of children's experiences of separation from parents, I would have thought it should have been better to be at least with one parent, as we were, but the cruelty of the village children was to make my life there really awful.

We were teased, ridiculed, blamed and even told, 'Go back to London

Soldiers, civil-defence workers and civilians clear the debris as they search for survivors amid the ruins of a school hit during a daylight raid on the London area.

and be gassed.' (There was a threat of gas being used against Britain.) One village boy contracted ringworm and we were told that 'dirty London' must have given it to him. One girl at school used to play ball with me after school, but ignored me in the class, denying to the others that she played with me.

The old lady we lived with was quite kind, and the parts I enjoyed were 'wooding' (collecting firewood) with two elderly women, and once going to see a Sonja Henie film about ice-skating 12 miles away in Stony Stratford. I saw women making lace on their front steps, with large pillows and bobbins. I look back on that with a sense of privilege.

Some weekends at night my mother would take us to a high part of the village and we could see the searchlights in the far distance. We thought of my dad and cried.

I learned to do joined-up writing in the communal classroom, children aged five to eleven in one room. There was a coal fire in the winter, and some children were given a spoonful of Virol every morning.

One day a girl bit me and told Mrs Griffin, the headmistress, that I had bitten her. I was made to wear a placard round my neck that day saying 'I am a dog'. That school was the worst time of my life. We were there for two years. I still don't like going away from home.

Joy MacRae with her mother and three brothers while they were evacuees in St Albans, Hertfordshire.

Joy MacRae (now Fox) moved away from the danger area with her mother and brothers, and continued to be on the move for some time.

Mum and the four kids were evacuated together, but the hardships were perhaps more difficult owing to the fact that we were forced to live in one-room accommodations (at several different locations) and perform all of our daily functions in that room, including toilet, eating and sleeping – all in one bed of course.

I was four when the war started in 1939, and we lived in pleasant surroundings in Ashford, Middlesex [just outside London]. I remember only a little about that house, but I do remember it was nice there; we had a proper kitchen, bedrooms, an Anderson shelter in the garden and nice neighbours. There were many nights when we slept in the Anderson shelter, sometimes with neighbours, sometimes not, but always with the smell of the earth, oppressive. I can still remember the feeling that the earth would cave in and bury us alive. I can't bear being in tunnels which go under the water, and I can't stand the feel of earth on my hands – hangovers perhaps?

I recall one night when an incendiary bomb fell on a neighbour's house, although I don't know during what period it was. The real bombing started in 1941 I believe, but whenever it was, we seemed to be on the

*er home – and her
e – destroyed by a
mb, a little girl
ngs to a rescue
orker.*

edge of the action, but getting caught in it nevertheless. Our house received a hit one night when we were all in the shelter. Mum and her four kids were without a home of our own for the next few years, moving about from one evacuee refuge to the next when the house-owners tired of our company.

I recall we were sent to St Albans, in Hertfordshire, away from the action – or perhaps that was where there was room for us. I will never know for sure.

What followed for us were several terrible years. The one-room haven which was our home became also our prison. There was no privacy for five people living together in one room, sleeping in one bed, using one bucket as a toilet, eating from a packing-case. We stayed until the owners tired of us and then we had to move on, like gypsies, instead of the respectable people we were.

The second address to which we were sent was owned by an old man who only lived in the bottom half of the house. I recall that this house was behind the Odeon cinema in St Albans, and I recall his name too. He was dirty and unkempt, and his house was dirty. We were 'allotted' an upstairs room, but it was an unhappy stay and we were constantly locked out of this house. He just didn't want us there. The final straw came when he would not let us in to get our possessions, and Mum had to get the police to bring a ladder, which we put to the upstairs window and got our clothes and meagre belongings out.

There was one more stay in St Albans, over the Christian Science Reading Room on the London Road. This place seemed to have people in similar circumstances: we were all getting second-hand clothes and none of us had enough to eat and we were all tired of being pushed around. My greatest pleasure was looking at the animals in the pet shop next door.

I recall an incident when we were living in St Albans. I was at some kind of nursery school, out for a walk, and we had been given stubs of pencils in a 'Monet' blue shade which I loved. I truly wanted this pencil, even though it was chewed and stubby, and I tucked it into my hand-knitted knickers! Of course, it fell out owing to the looseness of the fabric, and the teacher (or leader) found it and put me over her knee in front of the class, took down my woolly knickers and spanked my bare bum! I was mortified, and peed myself there and then. I've never forgotten the injustice of that incident. That woman never should have been in charge of children.

My father had left the family when we lived in Ashford and had gone off with another woman to live in London. It was doubly difficult for my mother without a husband to support her, and she was forced to be both

Mrs Shepherd with
er seven children in
double Anderson
helter.

Taking refuge in a
London Underground
station.

Above: *Parents and children inspect the hole left by a bomb that hit the Waifs and Strays Office in Kennington Road, London, bursting a water main and flooding the shelter. All 153 people inside the building were rescued.*
Left: *When it came to filling sandbags, everyone joined in – men, women and children. Apart from anything else, it was easier on the nerves than sitting still and wondering just how long it would be before bombs started falling.*

Right: *Civilians helping police to carry the wing of a German plane which fell near Victoria, London after being shot down during a raid in September 1940.*

parents for many years. (My father never did seem to want to face up to his responsibilities, i.e. the children and the cost of maintaining them – she took him to court on many occasions to get her alimony from him.) She worked at many menial jobs to support us: packing fish, factory work, cleaning houses and offices – whatever came along, that's what she did. Her comfortable life as an army officer's wife had not prepared her for career-type work.

Eventually we left St Albans to go down to her sister's house in Rowhedge, in Essex. Her sister already had eight children, and even though by this time my brother Colin was in the Fleet Air Arm, it was still a very crowded house in Rowhedge. I hated living there. We used to sleep under the Morrison table in the main room of the council-owned home. I should mention that bedridden Grandmother was also there, and sometimes I slept in her room. The lights stayed on and people talked; it was difficult to sleep. I am a light sleeper to this day, the slightest noise awakens me, but whether I can attribute it to the social meetings in my grandmother's room, or to disturbances of the wartime activity, I don't know.

I recall that when we lived in Rowhedge, the Americans came to England, and many of the older local girls were going out with the 'Yanks'. I used to hang around and watch, because I knew they would give me some gum to go away! I listened to a lot of talk about the things that Americans did that English boys didn't – ah well, I know better now, it's the same the world over!

Another incident which took place in Rowhedge had very tragic results. The house backed on to government-owned fields – known locally as 'the Governments'. There were marvellous blackberries to be had on this property, although we were not supposed to go in there, for it was here that the Army practised with their shells, bullets and bombs, and they kept a red flag flying when they were practising. But what do little kids know of that? One day my two brothers, Ian and Alan (about eleven and eight respectively), went out to collect blackberries with cousin Peter (he was around ten I believe). They all arrived back before lunch with a sack which Alan had carried on his back. The sack was dumped at the top (or bottom) of the garden and left there for examination by the boys after lunch.

I had watched their return and wanted to be included in any activity, so called my mum's attention to their treasure during lunch. Lunch was just ending, and I was being mean and sneaky because they wouldn't let me go up the garden with them. I called my mum to come outside, and I was about to run up the garden, when a mighty blast shook the house and broke the windows. I saw my brother kneeling and screaming, with blood coming in spurts out of holes in his body. My cousin was blown apart. My brother Alan had lain down with a pain in his side (due to carrying the sack no doubt), and this I believe saved his life.

Ian spent a long time in hospital, and for many, many years had shrapnel coming out of his body. He was a very lucky boy that day. The bomb was a Mills bomb, and my brother Alan, aged eight, had to go to an inquest and describe exactly what they had picked up. I recall that he was commended for his literate description of the bomb in question and even drew a picture for the presiding magistrate.

Life was difficult in Rowhedge after that, understandably so, and when Mum got a chance to rent a condemned cottage in Wivenhoe (just across the river), she did so. It was our own place – even though it was filthy, had rats, mice, bedbugs, cockroaches, spiders, no toilet facilities or running water, and the cooking facilities consisted of one single gasring on the floor right inside the front door! The toilet was at the bottom of the garden and consisted of a wooden building which we shared with a neighbour. Every winter it froze, and I got used to going to the toilet at school rather than testing the outdoor facilities. I believe Mum paid one shilling per week for this terraced cottage, which had been condemned for many years. We lived there until we emigrated to Canada in 1958.

Eileen Williamson (now Challis), who lived in Custom House, near London's Royal Albert Dock, stayed in the capital throughout the war. She watched as other children prepared to be evacuated:

All the children had labels on their coats going around to Hallsville School, E16. A lot of them went during the day and were going by coaches from the school. It got dark, so a lot of children had to stay in school till morning. It had a direct hit, and all the children were killed. We lived just at the back of the school. They dug for three days and three nights and then put lime down. They built a new school on top after the war, and a sign hangs in the school saying how many children lost their lives.

We did not go, thank goodness, and we stayed all through the war in E16. We were bombed out three times, and saw so much bombing.

In 1940 we went hop-picking down in Kent for two weeks. When we came back, our street, Maplin Road, was empty. There was no one, only ARP wardens, who used to come and see if we were OK at night in our Anderson shelter.

I think it was the Blitz then. I had no friends. I used to collect all the cats that were left in an old pram, with an old net curtain over so they could not run away, then feed them and put them in an old house that was

'G is for gas-mask . . . A wartime lesson at Creek Road School in South East London.

138

Above: *After a night of heavy bombing, parents and children in Swansea are more than ready for tea and sandwiches from a mobile canteen.*
Left: *Buns and tea from a Paddington air-raid kitchen for children who have been bombed out of their homes in Lewisham, South East London.*

empty. My poor mum tried her best to feed them.

We never saw any of our neighbours come back; they had no homes left. I remember it was like a ghost town.

As the year wore on, many of the parents who had resisted the initial call for evacuation, or had brought their children back to the cities, decided that they had made a mistake. Once again, thousands of people boarded buses and trains and headed for the countryside.

Doreen Miller (née Cooper), who was evacuated along with her elder sister, remembers one incident in particular from the end of 1940:

A British War Relief Society label that was attached to a gift – a picture book, knitting needles and wool – sent to Doreen Cooper from the USA one Christmas.

It was Christmas. She was eleven and I just seven. Our foster mother (I now know she should never have been allowed near children) used to have a variety of male 'cousins' visiting her at night. They ate our rations, while we were fed on potatoes and swedes, which we were made to steal from the local farmers' fields in the dead of night.

Well, just before Christmas this particular visitor arrived with a pocketful of unbelievable luxury – mince pies. The poor, unfortunate man was blind, and my heart went out to him as I watched, with mouth watering, as he tried to put the crumbled mince pies back together.

About ten years ago I said to my sister, 'Do you remember that poor blind man who brought mince pies to us at Mrs Pearce's house?' She roared with laughter and said, 'He wasn't blind, he was drunk.'

The innocence of a seven-year-old!

7
ESCAPE
ACROSS
THE
OCEAN

The growing threat of German invasion spurred the Government into studying new ways to encourage evacuation. Offers of help from private citizens in the Dominions and the United States led to the establishment of the Children's Overseas Reception Board (CORB), the corner-stone of a scheme enabling children between the ages of five and sixteen attending grant-aided schools to go abroad for safety.

Margaret Beal was one of those who benefited from the scheme. At the age of fifteen, she travelled from her home in Scarborough, Yorkshire, to Canada. She kept a record of her experiences in a diary:

Long queues formed outside the Passport Office in Westminster as thousands of people applied for permits to send their children and other relatives to Canada.

Sunday August 4th, 1940
Set off from Scarborough at 10.55 a.m. Mummy and Daddy were very brave. We went to York and changed there. In my carriage were Olga Burrows, Jeanne Gaunt, Teddy and Maurice Hayes (I knew all these beforehand) and some smaller children. We had a fairly long wait on York station, but finally we got our small luggage into a carriage and

Youngsters applying to be evacuated to the Dominions undergo a medical examination in a London school, June 1940.

started for Liverpool. We ate our dinner, but didn't want much, because it was so hot. We were boiled on the journey, and bored stiff. When we went through the Pennine Chain, we kept passing through tunnels which were miles long. It was annoying, being kept in the dark.

Finally we reached Liverpool, about 4.45 p.m., and waited on the platform while our luggage was taken out of the train and put into vans. We were bundled into buses and taken to a boys' school, where the boys were left. Our luggage was checked, and a bus took us to the corresponding girls' school. We were taken into a classroom, which had been converted into a dorm, and given beds. Olga and Jeanne are on either side of me. The beds are about four feet long. We went and had tea, and then we were sent out into the quad to play. Then we had prayers and went to bed, after washing the little ones.

The beds were awful. Jeanne and I didn't get to sleep till about 12 o'clock.

Monday August 5th, 1940
We were very tired in morning, after being up nearly all night, had a nice breakfast, after which we were examined by a nurse. I and the others were OK. Then we had our luggage checked. In the afternoon we three had a sleep, and then after a long long wait we were examined by two doctors, one doctor English and one Canadian. We were all passed. Then we had tea, and went to bed early, after pulling our beds together and placing another along the bottom of them to make room for our feet. We all slept well.

Tuesday August 6th, 1940

Got up this morning at 8.25; this was because Jeanne's watch went one hour slow. Never have we got washed and dressed so quickly, but we were in time. Breakfast wasn't very nice. The Childwall Valley girls gave us two plays, one a fairy one and the other Chinese. They were quite good. Dinner was fairly nice. In the afternoon all those over twelve went to a cinematograph show in the physics lab. There were four school films. The first, *Letters to Liners*, showed us how letters get to ships. The second was *The Life of a House-Fly*. The third was *Climbing Mount Tupper*, and the fourth and last, *Animals of the Sea*. We had a big tea and then we all went for a walk, and saw an old church which is very beautiful. At night we went and played ping-pong and then went and had

A page from Margaret Beal's diary.

n, and we three had a sleep; & then after a long
long wait we were examined by two
doctors, one doctor English, & one Candian.
We were all passed. Then we had tea,
and went to bed early after pulling our
beds together, & placing another along the
bottom of them to make our room for
our feet. We all slept well.

Tuesday. aug. 6th. 1940.
Got up this morning at 8.25; this was
because Jeanne's watch went 1 hr. slow.
Never have we got washed & dressed
so quickly, but we were in time. Breakfast
wasn't very nice. The Childwall Valley
girls gave us two plays, one a fairy
& the other Chin...

Children leaving for the USA wave to their parents on the balcony before their departure, August 1940.

supper with the other older girls. Went back to dorm, expected kids to be asleep, but no such luck. We tried to sing them to sleep with lullabies, but instead of making them sleep, they only asked for more. Slept solidly all night when at last I got off, but one of the children was very naughty, and kept us awake.

Wednesday August 7th, 1940
Got up and had a hot shower, we soaped ourselves and got very clean. Had breakfast, quite decent. Then we tidied our beds, and then went into the quad and finished writing a letter to Mummy and Daddy which I had begun in bed. We had to run round after our helper a bit, she won't do a darned thing for herself. We had dinner, and kept asking our helper to take us out – we meant town, but she thought otherwise, and lugged us out for a walk. Jeanne bought some choc. biscuits at an inn. Came home and had tea. After tea, a helper asked us three to clear the tables, which we did, setting them for breakfast afterwards. Then we went and mucked about in the ping-pong room, and then went and had some supper, which was only cold Ovaltine, because everyone else had guzzled everything, and then we went to bed. This morning they took every cent we had away from us, and put it in an envelope with our names on, and if we want any, you must ask the helper for it. They wouldn't even leave us a copper or two. We had an air-raid warning.

Thursday August 8th, 1940
This morning we knew definitely that we were leaving, though we had a jolly good idea before. But nobody seemed to know where, though they said that it would be a long journey. We got up fairly early, and washed and dressed. After breakfast we folded our beds and blankets up, and packed our cases. Then we waited for ages in the corridor, and finally got into buses which carried us to the station. Here, we were put into dining

cars, the boys were a couple of coaches along, but we were not allowed to see one another, anyway, the boys trotted along to see us. We have got to know some other boys as well. For dinner, they gave us bottles of milk and LMS [London, Midland and Scottish] luncheon boxes. These were lovely, and contained two meat sandwiches, a pork pie, a bun, a banana and a packet of chocolate. In the afternoon we three all had a little sleep, and then we read and talked until the train drew in at a rather small station, where we were met by officials, and were put into lovely buses, which carried us to a tremendous school. We were put in one half, and the boys in the other half. When we had got our outdoor clothes off, they stood us a most marvellous tea. Soup, salad, meat, and plenty of bread and jam. After tea we wandered around the school a bit, and then went to bed.

The beds were simply marvellous. They were very low, but had *springs*. Gosh! What a difference from before. Over us we had three very soft warm blankets and, glorious, a pillow. But best of all, they were about six feet long. At 8.30 p.m. we went to the dining room and were given a bottle of milk and biscuits.

Finally, we turned in, and spent an extremely comfortable night.

Friday August 9th, 1940

Woke and got up very early in morning. Got dressed as best we could, because all the small children were very interested, had a wash and then went into breakfast, which was delicious. Went back and folded our blankets up and put all our clothes ready to put on. When we finally got the word to set off, we got ready and had new labels tied on, then we waited for quite a long time in the passage, and moved on a bit, only to have another long wait. During the second wait the Provost of Glasgow and Mr Geoffrey Shakespeare [the director of the CORB programme] came up to see us. We were singing songs, and finally we got into buses and were taken to Glasgow station and were put on to the boat train. Everybody looked at us as we went along the street, and we waved to everybody.

The boat train took us to Greenock and we went past some men; one of them pulled half of our new labels off and read out our surname, and another ticked us off on a bit of paper. We then went aboard the tender. It was blowy weather, but we stood on deck and watched the land get further and further away. Finally we pulled alongside the liner, which is called *Antonia*. I am in a teeny weeny cabin, with Jeanne and two very tiny girls. It is not a very big ship, but a very nice one. There are a lot of nice boys aboard.

They feed us marvellously, and our waiter is very nice. Four of the

*...acuees bound for
...stralia embark on
...ir ship – and on a
... way of life.*

girls in our group sit at table one. The bunk is very comfy and I had a good night's rest. We have lifeboat drill and must not move without our gas-masks.

Saturday August 10th, 1940
Micky, the man who cleans our cabins, knocked us up at 6.30 a.m. We had asked him to do this the previous night and he made such a row that he woke the whole corridor up.

We got dressed and had a nice breakfast, after which we tidied our cabin and then had a practice of 'action stations'. We walked about the ship and talked to people until 12 o'clock, when we had a delicious lunch. After lunch we all came to the ladies' rest room, where I wrote a letter to Mummy and Daddy. We had dinner, and after that we went around and got a lot of autographs, then went to bed.

Sunday August 11th, 1940
Got up about 6.30 and went to Communion with Olga. It was a nice service, because the padre is very nice. Then we went up on deck, and to our surprise the ship started moving. We sat up on deck most of the day. Olga was sick and Jeanne played around with some boys, to my great amusement.

Monday August 12th, 1940
Got up and went on deck. It was raining. Divided my attention all day between the deck, the lounge and the square. I felt a bit woggly, and spent a bad night; had a sore throat.

Tuesday August 13th, 1940
Woke up in morning and nurse came in. Told her my throat was sore, whereupon she made a face and took my temperature, telling me to go to surgery at ten o'clock. Anyway, when the time came, I was fast asleep, and they didn't bother me. About two o'clock I woke up and came on deck, where I stayed until bed-time. It rained most of the afternoon, but I was fairly warm. Had a good night.

Wednesday August 14th, 1940
Got up and felt rotten. Didn't want to move, but they made me go up on deck. Felt a bit better up there and had a sleep, had half an apple and luckily didn't bring it up straight away. Spent all day up on deck; it was bed-time when we came in.

Thursday August 15th, 1940
Stayed on deck all day, very hot, went to bed early. Got out of physical jerks.

Friday August 16th, 1940
Washed children in morning, because Jeanne didn't feel well. Didn't have any breakfast, but had a bit of lunch and dinner. Stayed on deck all day, and got out of physical jerks.

Saturday August 17th, 1940
Got up and did a lot of ironing for all our section. Then darned a sock for a boy. Stayed on deck and played about all day. At dinner we were given paper hats and marvellous food – turkey and two and a half puddings, and two ice-creams. We get a lot of ice-cream here. Everybody got sort of silly because they had silly hats on, and we had some grand fun. Went to a cinema show, but it was awfully hot and the pictures weren't very good,

being silent and very old-fashioned. Went on deck after to get cooled down. It was very nice and the moon was over the water.

Sunday August 18th, 1940
Got up at 6.30 and went to Communion with Olga. Stayed up on deck most of day, got out of PT. We three washed our hair in afternoon; it was a great relief to do it, as our hair was very salty and sticky. It was absolutely boiling hot all day. We also went to children's service in the afternoon. Later in the afternoon, a whole gang of us went into the lounge and played about, and some of the boys were taking the electric bulbs out. Mrs Thomas took us on deck for a lovely drink of orangeade. It had ice and a cherry and a piece of orange in it. The moon was over the water, and it looked very beautiful. We went in about 10.30.

Monday August 19th, 1940
Got up and after breakfast, did some washing and then washed three of the kids' hair for them. I packed my case and had a bath. In the afternoon we stayed up on deck and sighted land. It was very hot. At last we drew into Halifax, and imagine our joy when a newsreel cameraman came aboard and took our pictures. Then suddenly, they told us that we had an hour to get off. Some of us hadn't had dinner, and we dashed down to get it. We had to put half-dry clothes into our cases and all other odds and ends. What a rush. Then we disembarked, and went into the customs house, where we stayed until about 12 p.m. having some milk and biscuits to keep us going. We were very tired when we finally got on to the train and undressed and went to 'bed' – two seats facing one another and then let down. Jeanne slept with me and we had a very comfy night. The train set off about 1.30 a.m. The cars were very big, and there are bunks above our heads which let down.

Tuesday August 20th, 1940
Woke up this morning and got dressed. We think that we are staying at Winnipeg, anyway, we know that we are going there. Some are going to Vancouver, and some to Montreal. They put up little tables between the seats and we had breakfast of bacon, cereals, bread and marmalade, and about ¾ pint of milk. Everybody waves to us as we go past, and when we stop in the stations, people come and talk to us and give us presents and sweets galore. We are passing a lot of water, and we have just seen a lot of wood logs in a lake. There is wood, wood, everywhere, and all the houses are made of it. Over the other side of the water there are big pine woods, with a few deciduous trees. All the people over here talk so nicely. A lady has just come along asking me about names, and I am pretty sure

that we are going to Winnipeg. We were talking to some men in a dining car of a train which was drawn along beside us, and they threw about six peaches in to us. We are always seeing soldiers, and sometimes their trains draw alongside ours, whereupon we talk to them. Lots of them give us sweets and things, and when we move away they all wave and stick their thumbs up, and we do the same. We have nice meals in enamel dishes and they fix little tables up between the seats. We went through Quebec, and saw all the lights twinkling across the water, it all looked very beautiful. We have passed through towns in which French is spoken, and some little boys passed the carriage in one place and Jeanne said, 'Do you speak English?' and they laughed and said, 'Non.' Then some girls passed and I said, 'Parlez-vous Francais?' and they laughed and shouted, 'Oui.' In Quebec we talked to two nice Frenchmen. A lady also came along with a whole box of chocolate and doled it out, and a little

Miles from home, and still miles to go . . . Children evacuated to Canada pass through Bonaventure station in Montreal on their way to Toronto.

boy brought along a lot of lollipops. Then we went into Montreal. We wanted to keep awake and see it, but we couldn't. Some children got out there though, poor things, it was about midnight when we got there.

Wednesday August 21st, 1940
Woke up this morning to be told by Jeanne that I had been talking in my sleep. Got up and had a nice breakfast. It was a sunny day contrary to yesterday's rain. We are passing a great lot of water and the trees, which come right down to the water's edge, make it very beautiful. This morning we came through Ottawa; we make a lot of stops in this journey which is a nuisance, because it takes us longer to get there. Just read and talked all day. In the morning I had a sleep because I was very tired. I had toothache, and one of the nurses put some oil of cloves on it, ugh, it did taste awful. I slept on the other side of the bed and didn't spend a very good night.

Thursday August 22nd, 1940
Woke up fairly early this morning, and tried to kill time, only to be put back again earlier than ever, because of changing the time. Had a nice breakfast and then read and tidied my small case up a bit. We expect to reach Winnipeg about 3 p.m. I rather hope we stay there, because people say it is a nice place, and I am rather tired of travelling. It was very, very hot in the carriage, and we were bored stiff, and couldn't find much to do. Finally we reached Winnipeg. There were people on the platform to see us, of committees and things, and there were newspaper men who took our pictures. A man came into our carriage and read out our names. Jeanne's and Olga's came together, and then a boy's name, and I was frightened that mine wouldn't be read out, but it was just after the boy's name. Then we waited on the platform a bit, and talked to some of the people, soon after that waving the boys and girls off who were going on to Edmonton and Vancouver. Then we went out of the station and had our pictures taken, and then got into the motor buses, which took us to a beautiful school, which is for deaf and dumb people. We were given beds, and we hung our coats up. Then for a while until supper we played about in the grounds; after supper we read magazines, then had a bath and went to bed. We don't quite know how long we will be parked here. By the way, it seems that the people were told that we were passing through all the stations, and that's why they were all there to see us.

Friday August 23rd, 1940
Got up, washed and dressed, then had breakfast, at which I served. Went for a walk round the grounds and then all of us went over to the park. It is

Love from your own Margaret. xx

Margaret Beal, aged 15, in Winnipeg, Canada, speaks to her parents back home in Yorkshire, England via the radio on Christmas morning 1940.

*1943 Margaret's
other, Jean (centre),
as flown out to
anada in secret to
ppear as the mystery
uest on the television
ow* Flashback *on
others' Day.
Margaret (left) was
bsolutely
umbfounded when
er mother appeared.
hey are pictured
ith their television
ost, Paul Soles.*

very beautiful. There is a zoo, with lions and bears and monkeys and wolves and other things. There is also an English garden. We saw a humming-bird moth. Then we went to the pavilion, and bought fruit ices for a nickel. They were lovely. Then back home for dinner, and after that, in the afternoon, we went aboard buses, which took us to the children's hospital for *another* medical exam. It is funny, all the traffic and steering wheels are on the different side of the road from those in England. We took all our clothes off, except our 'bloomers', as the nurse called them, and put on little sort of white coats. We were weighed and measured, and then went one by one to a doctor and a nurse. There were two or three couples doing us. I went in to the doctor, who was very nice. He asked me about everything, and examined me, and then said, 'She seems to be disgustingly healthy.' When he came to mental condition, he said, 'What shall I put?' and I said, 'Oh, 'weak,' and he laughed and put 'bright'. There was nothing wrong with me. Most of the girls were innoculated for diphtheria, even those who had been done before, but I wasn't, but we were all done for TB. In fact it was a very rigorous exam.

Then back we came in the buses to the school. It was fun driving through the city and seeing all the shops. By the way, as we entered the bus, we were all given new hankies. Coming back, we were given the newspapers with our photos in, they are very good. It was funny, on the platform I said to someone that Peter Parsons was a brat. Evidently the person to whom I said this was a reporter, because in the *Winnipeg Free Press* it said, 'Little Margaret Beal, who had taken Peter Parsons, aged 6 (he is 11), under her wing during the journey, said she would rather stand five million bombs than Peter for one hour, but there was a smile on her face as she said it.' I never said any such thing, gosh! would I like to know where he got it from.

Unfortunately, hardly had the overseas evacuation scheme begun when the *City of Benares* was sunk by a U-boat off the coast of Ireland as it headed for Canada. Seventy-three evacuees lost their lives. The CORB programme was immediately brought to a close.

*British evacuees in
New York: above,
children dancing
round the maypole,
and opposite, the little
Bloom twins dressed
as Uncle Sam and
John Bull, June 1942.*

8
THE
BOMBING
CONTINUES

Meanwhile, in Britain, there was no let-up in the bombing. From 1940 onwards, not only London but other cities also became German targets. Many parents who had sent their children away for safety now reassured themselves with the thought that maybe they had made the right decision – in spite of the heartache. Others, who had chosen to keep their families at home, decided that their children might be better off in the countryside after all.

Despite her efforts to drag her widowed mother away from the evacuee notices posted on the school gateposts, seven-year-old Brenda Jones (now Adkins) soon found herself one of a large group of Coventry children who were being sent away:

A little girl wearing one of the brightly coloured gas-masks for toddlers, with red rubber and blue enamel.

I was a very shy child, and the thought of leaving my mother terrified me. However, early one morning I was put on a coach, clutching a small suitcase, my gas-mask and a doll called Peggy.

I didn't know a soul, and as my mother waved goodbye I felt panic-stricken, but all the other children were singing at the tops of their voices, 'Hang out your washing on the Siegfried Line,' so I sat in silent anticipation through what seemed to be miles of countryside.

The most distant place I'd heard of on the radio was France, so I thought this must be our destination. In fact we were delivered to Coleshill Town Hall, between Coventry and Birmingham (about ten miles from Coventry). Here, we all sat on our suitcases while lots of pleasant motherly ladies bustled around collecting and disappearing with small groups of children. I thought no one wanted me, but eventually a farmer's wife took five of us to the village of Lea Marston. Three children

The farmhouse in Lea Marston where Brenda Jones was billeted.

The ruins of Coventry Cathedral after the raid in 1940.

went to other villagers and a boy called Carl and I remained at the farm.

I thought this was great as I loved animals. It was such a different world to me, going from a little terraced house with my mother and brother being bombed nightly to a very large detached house in quiet surroundings with extensive grounds, with a maid (who caused us to giggle by singing as she scrubbed the floor), a gardener, cowhand, shepherd and a gentleman farmer and his wife who always called him 'Teddy Darling' and, most impressive of all, all those gorgeous animals.

I felt quite excited and happy to be evacuated. I still have a postcard somewhere from the farmer's wife to my mother asking for my dressing gown and slippers. My mother duly obliged, but I don't know how, because I didn't have any; and getting hold of them in wartime Britain must have been difficult.

We were to experience more air raids, however, as the farm was near Hams Hall Power Station and the Germans tried to incapacitate it by showering it with incendiary bombs.

As travelling was rather difficult, I was visited only occasionally by my mother and brother. Sometimes he cycled and sometimes my uncle would manage enough petrol from his funeral business (a very necessary occupation in those days) to visit. I was always delighted to see them, but they were becoming less familiar to me as time went by. My mother took me home before the end of the war, as she was upset because I seemed to be forgetting her. On reflection, it's amazing how resilient and adaptable children are.

One night which stands out in my mind was a very noisy one with concentrated bombing, loud explosions and a deep red glow in one area of the sky. It went on for so long that most of the villagers stood outside watching. The significance of the situation must have escaped me until a neighbour thoughtlessly said, 'That's Coventry burning – there won't be a soul left alive there by tomorrow.' They must have seen the look of horror on my face, as I was rushed indoors with explanations that the direction of the glow was Birmingham, not Coventry. In fact it was Coventry, enduring the notorious April blitz. Although many people died, all my family – including grandparents, aunts, uncles and cousins – escaped unharmed.

I loved the village school, where a lot of time was spent on home crafts such as sewing, embroidery and knitting socks for the armed forces. We also went on a blackberry expedition around the fields and picked basketfuls of berries to help the food shortage. My academic work was so far behind the city standard when I returned that I found it difficult to catch up.

Altogether, it was an experience I dreaded but which I wouldn't have missed.

Rosalie Diamondstone (now Newman) was evacuated from Leeds in September 1940:

My mother took me to school, as usual, but instead of going inside, I joined all the other children lining up in the schoolyard. Gas-masks slung over our shoulders, we were marched off to a nearby school, *en route* passing the street on which I lived. Excited with anticipation of adventure, I waved to the neighbours and my mother, who walked on the opposite side of the street till we reached the next school, where another mass of children waited in neat line-ups in their schoolyard.

The great adventure began as my classmate and I boarded a bus and blew kisses to our mothers, who now, standing close to the side of the bus, pressed their faces to the window. Though separation began the moment our bus pulled away, the implication of what it meant wasn't clear until we arrived in the country.

The bus pulled up in front of a crowd of people standing in the tree-shaded square, and one by one each child was taken away by an adult.

*A child injured in the
Blitz and sent to the
countryside to
recuperate is carried
by a nurse from car to
house in Bodmin,
Cornwall.*

The name of the village escapes me now, but I remember a friendly lady
approaching me and asking if I'd like to go home with her. To my utter
dismay, home turned out to be a farm. Fleeing the horror of so many
quacking, neighing and barking animals, I ran inside and lay sprawled at
the foot of the staircase leading to the bedrooms, sobbing.

With great understanding and gentleness, the lady coaxed me into telling her why I was crying. At first reluctant to answer, for fear of hurting
her feelings, I finally admitted to being afraid of the animals and said I
didn't want to stay there. So it was that she walked back with me to the
square, where a few people were still gathered, and I was taken home by
another lady, a Mrs Hood.

Mr and Mrs Hood and their four daughters, all older than I, made me
extremely welcome and within a short time I was a member of their
family. I went to the village school with the Hood girls, and also attended
a cheder (Hebrew school) especially set up for the Jewish evacuees.

The playground of my new school, unlike the one in Leeds, wasn't
paved. Ever the tomboy, I fell so frequently on the cinders that the
teacher in charge of first-aid supplies automatically asked which knee I'd
skinned every time I walked into his classroom, even when I'd been sent
there on an errand!

Mrs Hood wasn't quite so calm when she discovered blood on my
pillowcase one night as she came to tuck me in. Till then, I'd hidden that
day's escapade at a nearby unused water trough. Walking along the narrow lip, and balancing precariously, I'd lost my footing, clutched at one
handle, and brought the other down on my head.

There were nights when we woke to ack-ack noises, ran outside in dressing gowns and pyjamas, and looked up to a sky blazing with search-lights that swept and criss-crossed and occasionally illuminated enemy airplanes. It was ironic to realize in later years that the safe countryside to which I'd been evacuated was situated near an airbase.

My parents had no telephone and no car. The Hoods had no tele-phone, but Mr Hood rode a motor cycle with a side-car and on rare visits to Leeds would manage to see my parents and let them know I was well. A couple of times, my parents visited me at the Hoods, thanks to the generosity of a good neighbour and friend of theirs, who had a car.

Able to read and write prior to being evacuated, I loved getting letters from my parents. They'd left some paper, envelopes and stamps with Mrs Hood, and she made sure I wrote to them fairly regularly.

One letter-writing day I was feeling very homesick. Not wanting Mrs Hood to hear me cry, or see what I was writing, I ran out to the lavatory in the yard, with paper and pencil, and there proceeded to tell my parents that I was unhappy and wanted very much to come home. Despite any precociousness I might have had, I was naïve enough to hand my finished letter to Mrs Hood for mailing, without even realizing she would be able to read my secrets before putting them in the envelope she addressed, stamped and mailed.

How wise Mrs Hood was! Sitting me on her lap in the kitchen, she asked me if I wanted to make my parents very sad. Getting the expected negative response, she explained that they would cry if they read such a letter and suggested I rewrite it, just leaving out the part about being homesick. And that, of course, is exactly what I did.

Ultimately, Anderson shelters were installed in the cellars of those back-to-back row houses in Leeds, and my parents brought me home. It was great fun discovering a hole had been knocked out in all connecting cellar walls, so that in case of an emergency, we had basement access to my grandfather's house, next door, and through his to the next two in the row, as well as to all four connecting houses in the street behind us. Though at first we frequently used the cellar shelter during air raids, we fortunately had no need of the labyrinth cellar escape route.

My homecoming, late summer of 1941, was marred by nits that were quickly discovered by my mother, who vigorously attacked my hair and scalp with daily doses of vile-smelling substances, until the offending aliens had been obliterated. The problem was apparently widespread. Many children had unusually closely cropped hair or wore scarves on their heads, and school nurses carefully examined every child's head before they were permitted to return to school.

Improbable though others might find it, I am able to look back and say that despite the war, despite being separated from my family as an

*Bath-time at this
London County
Council nursery in
Berkshire clearly had
a far from dampening
effect on anyone's
spirits!*

evacuee and my father when he was in the RAF, I had a happy childhood. I was blessed with a loving family, the compassion of caring strangers, and wonderful friends who remain so today, and inherited some measure of the absolutely indomitable English spirit.

Having returned home from Hampshire to Battersea, in London, after the Blitz, Terry Law was then evacuated for a second time:

This time we went to Wales, to a little village called Llangadog. I can remember crying in the inevitable school playground as we were again picked out for a billet. What brought on the tears was that I couldn't decide whether to go with my mate Albie to a mansion or with my mate Don to a farm.

In the end I decided to go with Albie, and I must say I made the right decision. The mansion was called Glansevin, and I loved it. They had paintings on the walls, a telephone (Llangadog 8 was the number), several bathrooms, a smoking room and a kitchen so big we could ride round the table on our skates. There were lawns, vegetable gardens, stables, kennels for the hounds and even servants' quarters – all of whom had long since gone.

Glansevin was so big we used to put up airmen on leave. There were Poles, New Zealanders and Australians. I recall a bomber flying over the house very low several times – it must have been one of our visitors making a return trip. Although I loved the place I can remember crying at night because I missed my mum and dad.

Marjorie Williams (now Hole) was evacuated, but returned to Manchester during the bombing:

When I was back home with my mum, dad and little baby brother, whenever the sirens went we used to go to Mulberry Street School shelter. We used to have organized songs and dancing. There was a Yank and all his mates who used to come in and play his organ and have a party, and you got to know everyone.

The bombs came quite close. When it was all clear, lots of us kids collected shrapnel, bullets, anything we could find. On the way back home to our own house, we would see other houses on fire and wonder if we would lose a lot of friends or if they were in other shelters. Some were, some weren't, and if they had nowhere to live, my mum or someone would take them in. We had our house so overcrowded we were falling over each other, lending out coupons to each other for food or making a big pan of oxtails from the butcher.

*Some 200 infants –
many of whom had
lost one or both
parents in air raids –
were evacuated from
London's East End to
this country mansion,
fitted out as a nursery
by Lady Guston. They
are pictured having
tea and playing on the
lawns of their
beautiful new home.*

Queuing with bedding outside a London shelter, July 1944.

Right: A V1, or doodlebug, in flight over southern England, just before the engine cut out and it plunged to earth. Below: A doodlebug dives down over Piccadilly, London.

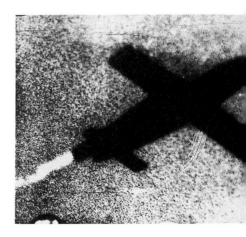

Examining the propulsion unit of a V2 rocket at Limehouse, London, March 1945.

In the years that followed, as the war progressed and Britain's armed forces abroad continued both to make advances and to suffer setbacks, at home on British soil the nation listened to the news – and waited. The air raids became more frequent and more widespread. Britain witnessed the welcome arrival of American, Polish and Commonwealth servicemen – and the not-so-welcome appearance of the terrifying VI, or doodlebug, and V2 rocket.

Children who had stayed in the cities, or gone back to them, sat tight, crossed their fingers and hoped and prayed as the enemy attacks intensified, while those who had been sent to the countryside for safety went on wondering how long it would be before they were reunited with their families.

Gradually, following the landing of Allied troops in France in June 1944, the danger from the air abated, and evacuees all over Britain began to return home. At last, on 7 May 1945, the German Supreme Command surrendered. The war was over, and it was safe for everyone to retrace their steps to the cities. By the time another year had elapsed, the official resettlement scheme was complete, and children everywhere had said goodbye to their foster parents and set off homewards.

For many evacuees, however, it was not to be goodbye for ever. They would not forget the people who had taken them in and the places that had been their homes for so long. And one day, some of them would go back.

9
GOING
BACK

Many evacuees have kept in contact with their foster parents, either by maintaining a written correspondence or by going to see them in person. The experiences of those who have revisited their wartime homes have differed widely. Some have returned to find that little has changed, others to discover that once-familiar places are now barely recognizable. But for all of them, going back has proved to be both memorable and nostalgic.

Eileen Watkins (page 34):

I continued to keep in touch with Mr and Mrs Hare and Auntie and Uncle. In 1960, whilst on holiday with my husband and children, we stopped in Castleton so I could show them where I had lived. As we had not received a card the previous Christmas I thought the worst had happened.

We walked over to the house and were greeted by the bark of a Pomeranian. Mr Hare had passed away in November 1959, but Mrs Hare was still there, very frail, sight failing, but mentally very alert at ninety years of age. My husband asked her to what she attributed her great age. She replied, 'A glass of Guinness at lunch-time and a port every night,' – and she used to tell us it was her medicine!! Sad to say, she passed away at the end of that year, so I'm glad for the reunion.

Auntie and Uncle spent two holidays at my mother's home after the war, and one at our home after my marriage. We emigrated to Australia in 1974 but still write to New Mills regularly. In 1982, my husband and I returned to England for a holiday, and one of our calls was to see Auntie. Unfortunately, Uncle had passed away in 1980. It was great to see her again. She looked so fit and well. The first thing that she said to me was, 'Do you know that it was 41 years ago today that you came to live with us?' I hadn't planned it that way, it was pure coincidence. She had moved from the house on the hill to a smaller home closer to town. At age 77, she is still very active with Church activities and the senior citizens' club. I only wish she could visit us here in Australia.

I have often asked myself why my foster parents chose me. I am glad they did. At the time I thought that my mother was cruel to send me so far away, but in later years I realize that like most mums she was doing what she thought best for her child. I am grateful that I had the chance to meet those wonderful people.

Joan Evans (page 97):

As I said, I went back again two years ago, and I saw the shop where I first stayed, but it was an antique shop now. So I entered, and was asked if I wanted something. I told the woman that I used to live there as a child. She looked a bit doubtful, so I described all the rooms and especially the loo, as one walked up five stairs and the throne was on top. That convinced her that I wasn't a 'con', so she invited me and my husband to go and have a look around. It brought back so many memories, but alas the place had deteriorated and I felt sad about that. Dunmow I remember with affection, and it hadn't changed too much.

I didn't mind being an evacuee. It taught me so much, and it was a happy time, and everyone was kind and all the kids seemed happy. Mrs Kirby took me to the cinema (just a sort of hut); I can remember seeing a Gracie Fields film. It's still standing, but closed down. So Dunmow hasn't changed much at all. I shall always remember it. The only thing that's changed is me. It seems a long time ago now, those days, but I can remember it as if it was yesterday.

Doreen Miller (page 141):

I have been reliving in my mind those four and a half years as an evacuee. There were bad times, but there were good times too. During that time I had one of the best teachers I have ever met. He was the headmaster of the village school, and he helped me learn two very important things – the love of reading and a deep and abiding love for the country and country things. As a young teacher in the '50s I went back to see him and learned from him the haphazard way that the children were placed in homes. He died a few years ago, but he will forever be alive in my heart, because of the kindly way he had with the evacuees under his care in his school.

Doreen Simson (née Ward):

I did not realize how lucky I was with the family that chose me, with whom I have always kept in touch by letter and gone to stay every few years. Over the years my foster mum always signed herself 'Mrs Sharpe' until 15 years ago, then it was 'Mum no. 2', and since I lost my own parents, it's been just 'Mum'. When I went to stay last year for a few days, she introduced me to her friends as her other daughter. I was very moved by that, as they are of another class of background to my own working-class one. I feel that my three and a half years with them shaped my future, leading to the florist job I have always had, and then my own flower shop, as they taught me all about flowers from the age of four – me not being used to them, coming from the White City estate in London.

Joan Wood (page 62):

My friend and I continued to keep in touch with our foster parents until Uncle Tom died, when we kept up the correspondence with Aunt Hannah until eventually the letters and Christmas cards from her stopped. Although I never saw them after I returned home, they sent me a present when I married in 1949 and a beautiful little nylon dress when I had my first baby, a little girl, in 1953. They must have been well into their eighties.

Although we missed our mums and dads and got homesick occasionally, they looked after us like their own, making us as happy as possible in the circumstances, and I remember them with great affection.

The late Valerie Benest (page 21 and page 74):

While on holiday in England last year I made a nostalgic visit to Lacock with my husband and youngest son. The village was unchanged except for visitors' cars; the kids were playing in the brook in exactly the same way that I remembered doing. A cricket match was taking place on the green. The local pub garden was full at lunch-time, and when I made enquiries at the local shop, the proprietor – now the daughter of the former owner – lapsed into the Wiltshire dialect and recalled the local names, most of whom were still the same names as all those years ago. Also on that green we used to play rounders as kids.

The cottage where I stayed had changed hands and has since been enlarged, but was otherwise as I remembered it. The old abbey is now open to the public, and I was able to add some titbits of information for the local ladies' group who provided the guide service.

I must say I was looked after and fed well while evacuated. I kept in touch with Auntie Hayden until she passed away a few years ago at the age of 92.

Doreen Chambers (page 82):

Every year, right up until I got married at 20, I went back to Lopen for my two weeks' holiday. (After two years, when I was nearly 14 and ready to go to work, I was given the choice of staying and being adopted by these folks, I had got so close to them, but the pull for my own family was too great, so hence my mother came down and I went back home to go to work in 1942.)

I honestly don't think the experience hurt me one bit. I have kept up correspondence with them ever since; Mrs Rowswell died last year at 84 years, and I am now carrying on the correspondence with her son Donald, who is just two years older than me. When we do get the chance to visit England, we always go to the village to visit everyone. The children who are married there now and still live in the village still remember me. I have only lovely memories of the unfortunate years. I have a 15-year-old myself now, and I can imagine the hurt that our parents must have gone through.

Terry Law (page 39 and page 166):

About 20 years ago I went back to Glansevin and took a photograph of the place. The house had not changed very much, although it was shabbier, with weeds growing in the main drive, and there was sacking up at some of the windows. The original owners, by the name of Lloyd, had long since moved away.

Looking at the photograph you will appreciate that moving from a terraced house in Battersea that backed on to a railway line was some move. The oak tree on the front lawn was great fun for climbing, and me and my fellow evacuee Albie Ellis spent a lot of time up there.

I understand the house is now a hotel, and I might just go down in the summer to see it and even stay the night.

Terry Law's photograph of Glansevin.

ACKNOWLEDGEMENTS

Only with the help of Roy Williams and Laurence Bradbury, the inimitable designers; Jenny de Gex, a wonderful picture researcher; Penny Phillips, my remarkable editor; and Doreen, my incredibly understanding wife, has it been possible to produce this book. It is my hope that the pages will remind all who turn them of the courage of children everywhere who, through no fault of their own, suffer the pain and confusion brought by war.